QuickBooks Online Mastery

[3 Books in 1] From Beginners to Experts, Achieving Financial Efficiency, Control, and Business Success for Small Enterprises

By

Jacob Wildes

TABLE OF CONTENTS

BOOK ONE

THE RIGHT APPROACH

Introduction

In the year 2023, QuickBooks stands out as highly favored accounting software among small enterprises. If one wants to transition from manual accounting, is burdened by the complexity of spreadsheets, or seeks an alternative to their existing software, QuickBooks presents itself as a cost-effective solution.

While QuickBooks is mostly recognized as bookkeeping software, it provides a diverse array of accounting and financial solutions tailored to the needs of small companies. The following are a few illustrative instances:

QuickBooks Payroll: This solution, offered in both self-service and full-service options, enables firms to reimburse a maximum of 50 workers using either check or direct deposit. In the event that you choose to avail yourself of a comprehensive service package, the computation and submission of your year-end W-2 tax documents for local, state, plus federal taxes are executed automatically.

QuickBooks Online: Accounting books may be stored on the cloud via the use of QuickBooks Online, enabling users to access them from any location and at any given moment. Additionally, this service can generate invoices.

QuickBooks Payments: QuickBooks payments facilitate the generation of pay-enabled invoices, establishment of recurring invoices, and enablement of digital payment reception while on the go. Customers have the option to make digital payments using their preferred method.

QuickBooks Commerce: The system consolidates all orders and inventory data into a centralized dashboard, providing users with up-to-date information on the progress of each order. QuickBooks Commerce has a high degree of scalability, enabling users to efficiently include additional sales channels or establish a B2B commerce platform while seamlessly integrating with various online marketplaces.

QuickBooks Live: By using QuickBooks Live, individuals have the opportunity to collaborate with a proficient bookkeeper who can assist in managing various aspects of their accounting requirements.

QuickBooks Time: QuickBooks Time facilitates the monitoring and documentation of billable hours for workers, customers, or projects. Tracking time and managing payments are simplified with the use of QuickBooks Payroll.

These applications exhibit a high level of integration with one another and the QuickBooks accounting software, therefore establishing a comprehensive accounting and payments environment suitable for small and medium-sized enterprises.

QuickBooks Online (QBO) is a cloud-based solution offered by Intuit. Rather than opting for a single payment, the user chooses a monthly subscription and only uses the secure web browser for accessing the program. Intuit provides frequent software upgrades and gives solutions to address issues. Nevertheless, the program also has pop-up advertisements promoting supplementary premium services.

Beginning of May 2014, QuickBooks Online was the leading online accounting software with a member base of 624,000, in contrast to Xero, a company that reported having 284,000 customers as of July 2014.

The cloud-based iteration of QuickBooks presents a distinct product in comparison to its desktop counterpart, showcasing a variety of capabilities that operate in a divergent manner.

In 2013, Intuit made an announcement stating that QuickBooks Online has undergone a complete reconstruction, emphasizing the implementation of a framework that facilitates customization of the online version of QuickBooks by customers and enables third-party developers to create small business apps.

Chapter 1: A Different Approach

QuickBooks Online is cloud-based accounting software developed and marketed by Intuit. It is designed to assist individuals and businesses in managing their financial transactions, such as invoicing, expense tracking and financial reporting,

QuickBooks Online is cloud-based accounting software designed to facilitate the management of many financial aspects for small companies, including accounting, income tracking, expenditure monitoring, payroll administration, and other related functions. Access to all accounts is facilitated by the online login interface, which encompasses various features such as personalized feeds and charts, the ability to create customized invoices, 'Pay Now' buttons, and mobile websites. Furthermore, these functionalities are equipped with automatic synchronization capabilities. The mobile applications designed specifically for iOS and Android platforms provide many functionalities, such as capturing sales receipts, monitoring expenses, managing cash flow, checking account balances, recording time, reviewing transactions, managing purchase orders, communicating with clients, and more.

QuickBooks Online facilitates the simultaneous access of comprehensive financial reports and accounts by many users with its feature of automatically synchronizing the whole of a business's financial profile onto a single dashboard. The program produces billing and invoicing solutions that are compatible with mobile devices and can be easily printed. Additionally, it provides profit, trade, and loss sheets. Individual users can create customized reports and feed inside the dashboard, enabling enterprises to only access the data that has the most significance for their operations.

QuickBooks Online provides customers with the ability to incorporate more users, modify permissions, and effectively monitor payments, invoices, sales history, and invoice particulars by means of the navigational interface. Intuit GoPayment, Shopify, QuickBooks Online Payroll, Salesforce, Xero, Square POS, and several more third-party programs have been seamlessly connected with QuickBooks Online.

1.1 The pricing structure of QuickBooks

The QuickBooks Desktop product range offered by Intuit has undergone an overhaul. Instead of offering one-time purchase licenses, QuickBooks now only provides Pro Plus and Premier Plus subscriptions for QuickBooks Pro and Premier. The purchase of a single QuickBooks Desktop license is no longer feasible.

The revised version and corresponding cost are shown below as of October 2022.

The availability of QuickBooks Desktop 2023 products has been established. There are no discounts available for desktop items, and the full manufacturer's suggested retail price (MSRP) is being charged across all distribution channels.

Desktop Version

QuickBooks Premier Plus	$799
QuickBooks Pro	$549

The cancellation of QuickBooks pricing is possible at any given moment. However, it is important to note that the service is charged on a monthly basis and does not offer the option of a refund or partial refund. Upon the termination of your subscription, it is also possible to refrain from generating additional transactions. However, there exists a provision to access and review run reports and accounting records for at least one year.

Payroll and time track pricing

There may be a requirement for the incorporation of supplementary features, such as payroll management and time-tracking capabilities. The table indicates the financial implications.

Version	Annually	Monthly
Elite	$2100	$175($125/month + $10/employee x 5 employees)
Premium	$1,380	$115($75/month + $8/employee x 5 employees)
Core	$780	$65($45/month + $5/employee x 5 employees)

Important: It is important to acknowledge that all of the QuickBooks Payroll plans encompass the following features:

- Automating the computation of tax payments and facilitating their computerized submission.

- The individual is responsible for the processing of both state and federal quarterly and yearly reports, as well as the preparation of W-2 and 1099 forms.

- The two methods commonly employed for compensating employees are issuing printed checks or utilizing direct deposit.

- The task at hand involves the processing of payroll for personnel who are employed inside the same state as the organization, as well as those who are employed in a separate state.

- One advantage of using QuickBooks Desktop Products is the ability to maintain current payroll tax tables without the necessity of installing updates.

- The utilization of the QuickBooks payroll mobile application facilitates many tasks, such as electronic payment of employee salaries, completing tax forms electronically, accessing prior paychecks, and making electronic tax payments.

In addition, the process of setting up QuickBooks payroll necessitates the inclusion of your bank account details and the provision of tax identification numbers. Before initiating a QuickBooks payroll subscription, it is imperative to ensure that you are adequately prepared to initiate payroll operations promptly.

QuickBooks subscription pricing

The online iteration of QuickBooks is offered in six distinct versions, each varying in price. It is common for individuals to select one or many versions according to their preferences and requirements. Please refer to the table provided next for the pricing information.

Version	Annually	Monthly	Users
Accountant	$0	$0	No limit
Advanced	$2400	$200	Up to 25 billable users + 3 accountant users
Plus	$1,020	$85	5 billable users + 2 accountant users
Essentials	$660	$55	3 billable users + 2 accountant users
Simple Start	$360	$30	1 billable users + 2 accountant users
Self-employed	$180	$15	1 billable users + 2 accountant users

QuickBooks offers users the option to select between fifty percent off for the initial three months of their chosen subscription or a complimentary 30-day trial period. There exists the potential for the provision of a discount to be extended to you during the duration of the 30-day trial period. Suppose you intend to utilize QuickBooks on an ongoing basis. In that case, it is advisable to subscribe to a plan, as there is no guarantee that a similar offer will be available after the trial time. The application of a 50 percent discount is a substantial chance for cost savings.

Additionally, the provision of a 30-day trial period allows users to evaluate the software's compatibility with their specific requirements without necessitating any financial obligations. In the event that one ultimately determines that QuickBooks is not suitable for their needs, they will be required to terminate their membership. However, it is important to note that the trial period will conclude on the thirtieth day.

Other add-on pricing.

QuickBooks Payments facilitates the utilization of electronic payment methods by consumers, hence obviating the need for conventional payment modes. Additionally, this service implies the imposition of per-transaction fees as opposed to monthly membership charges. The following table presents the prevailing rate at the time of composing this document.

Payment Type	Rate per Transaction
Keyed credit card	3.4% plus 25 cents (you will be able to enter the credit card information online)
Invoiced credit card	2.9% plus 25 cents (customers will be able to insert credit card online)
Swiped credit card	2.4% plus 25 cents (mobile reader available)
ACH Bank payments	1% up to a maximum of about $10 per transaction (with this, a customer inserts bank information online)

QuickBooks Payments facilitates the expeditious transfer of funds from eligible debit or credit card transactions to the designated bank account of the user on the subsequent business day. The payments with the deposit transactions would subsequently be recorded into your records automatically; however, this process is dependent on the funding date.

1.2 Comparing QuickBooks Features

QuickBooks incorporates a multitude of elements within its framework to enhance the user experience. In the subsequent sections, we will provide a concise discussion of the features above and their corresponding implications.

QuickBooks Simple Start

QuickBooks Simple Start provides bookkeeping functionalities. These functionalities enable business owners to enhance their ability to effectively oversee their billing, bookkeeping, and financial management.

The platform offers a unified online interface that enables users to conveniently obtain information, monitor their expenses and income, and generate invoices.

By using automation in these processes, the amount of time spent on administrative tasks can be significantly decreased. QuickBooks Simple Start is responsible for the digital storage of information. There is no longer a requirement to manually input business or client information on each occasion. Moreover, it has the potential to reduce the likelihood of human error.

QuickBooks Simple Start offers a wide range of bookkeeping functionalities. The services encompassed in this system include administration of 1099 contractors, generation of basic reports, estimating capabilities, management of receipts, tracking of income and expenses, monitoring of mileage, tracking of sales and sales tax, as well as facilitation of invoicing.

The utilization of QuickBooks Online for invoicing has several advantages, including the ability to easily customize and adapt the invoicing process, real-time monitoring of invoice statuses, expedited receipt of payments, and the provision of a user-friendly experience for customers.

QuickBooks effectively centralizes all receipts, facilitating the streamlined monitoring of business expenditures.

Self - Employed QuickBooks Online

It is recommended that independent contractors, such as real estate agents, Lyft and Uber drivers, and freelancers, utilize QuickBooks Self-Employed for their financial management needs. Users can securely log in to their accounts and access them from any computer that has an internet connection, similar to the functionality provided by QuickBooks Online.

The software possesses unique functionalities, such as the ability to monitor both business and personal expenditures from a single bank account and facilitate the transfer of data to TurboTax. These capabilities are not included in QuickBooks Desktop and QuickBooks Online. The calculation of your anticipated quarterly tax payments must be conducted, and you will be notified when they are scheduled to be paid.

Essentials of QuickBooks Online

QuickBooks Online Essentials is a software solution that enables businesses with a maximum of three individuals to effectively manage their accounts receivable, monitor their income and expenditures, as well as oversee their payables, which refer to the amounts owed to suppliers. Moreover, it facilitates the generation of accounts payable aging data, enabling users to effectively manage bill due dates. Furthermore, it is advisable to engage in effective communication with your accountant in order to streamline the complexities of the tax season.

The key differentiating factor between QuickBooks Online Plus and QuickBooks Online Essentials is the disparity in the number of users. While the Plus plan allows for a maximum of five users, the Essentials plan restricts the number of users to a maximum of three. The second factor to consider is the set of features that accompany each option. Furthermore, in addition to

the inclusion of inventory management functionality, which is highly advantageous for individuals engaged in sales activities, Plus also provides the capability to monitor and assess project profitability.

QuickBooks Online Plus

QuickBooks Online Plus is considered the most suitable accounting software for enterprises engaged in the sale of both goods and services. The enhanced package includes all the features provided by Simple Start and Essentials, in addition to advanced functionalities such as inventory cost and quantity tracking, purchase order creation, and project profitability monitoring. It includes the ability to track labor costs, expenses, and payroll using job costing. All of the capabilities above are accessible through the QuickBooks Online Plus platform. Furthermore, it is advisable to engage in communication with your accountant in order to streamline the complexities of the tax season.

QuickBooks Simple Start Usage limits

QuickBooks Element	Use Limit
Unbilled users	2 Accountant users for most plans, 3 for Advanced; unlimited reports - only users in plus and Advanced; Unlimited time tracking - only users in Essentials, plus, and Advanced.
Billed users	1 for Simple Start, 3 for Essentials, 5 for Plus
Classes and locations	40 combined; further, you cannot track your balance sheet by class.
Chart of accounts	250
Annual transactions	350, 000

The QuickBooks Simple Start, Essentials, and Plus editions impose strict limitations on the chart of accounts as well as the number of classes and locations. Once all available resources have been fully utilized, it becomes necessary to deactivate accounts, locations, or classes in order to create additional space. Alternatively, upgrading to an advanced membership is another viable option.

Essentials and Plus

Two of the available alternatives are the QuickBooks Essentials and QuickBooks Plus intermediate plans. The primary differentiating factor across QuickBooks Essentials and Plus lies in the target audience for which they are intended. Essentials are designed to cater to service-oriented enterprises that do not engage in the sale of physical products. The primary objectives of this system are to facilitate income tracking, bill and expenditure management, as well as payment collection.

In contrast, the Plus platform caters to organizations operating in the realm of products or services, offering functionalities such as project profitability management, purchase order creation, and inventory tracking. Furthermore, the inclusion of these advanced capabilities has led to a more refined reporting system.

Free mobile applications can be utilized to aid in the management of business operations while on the go, as they are integrated into the QuickBooks Online platform. In addition to the features above, each subscription plan encompasses automated processes, tailored reports designed to meet the specific needs of your organization, as well as automatic data backup functionality.

QuickBooks Online Advanced

QuickBooks Online Advanced is specifically designed to cater to the needs of businesses with intricate financial and accounting demands, rendering it the most powerful iteration of QuickBooks Online. QuickBooks Online Advanced provides enhanced insights, heightened tranquility, and improved productivity in order to prioritize significant decisions and progress to a higher level.

QuickBooks Online Advanced is a cloud-based accounting software designed specifically for firms that are experiencing growth and are of medium size. QuickBooks Online Advanced encompasses the fundamental accounting functionalities of QuickBooks, including a robust suite of tools such as customizable business analytics, tailored user roles for up to 25 individuals, revenue and cash flow dashboards, and online backup and restoration capabilities. The utilization of automated procedures and batch invoicing has been found to be advantageous in terms of time and cost savings. The mobile application enables employees to conveniently access real-time data from various places while also providing the functionality to track distance.

QuickBooks Online Accountant

The cloud-based software utilized for the management of accounting activities is commonly referred to as QuickBooks Online Accountant.

This software tool facilitates the inspection, editing, and correction of customer transactions for bookkeepers and accountants. After completing the registration process, accounting professionals are granted the opportunity to engage in the QuickBooks Online ProAdvisor program at no cost.

The QuickBooks Online Accountant platform offers a range of bookkeeping capabilities tailored to fit the demands of your company. It is specifically designed to work seamlessly with QuickBooks Online Advanced and includes several client tools to ensure comprehensive bookkeeping services.

The following are some of the most notable requirements of QuickBooks Online Accountants.

- The objective of this inquiry is to locate complimentary accounting practice administration software utilized by firms and accountants. QuickBooks Online Accountant, an accounting practice management software, stands out as a prominent choice due to its notable features. Notably, this program is available to accountants at no cost, which may initially appear implausible.

- Businesses who desire to effectively oversee the financial matters of their clients as well as their internal operations inside a unified platform: The software's adaptability allows for the comprehensive visualization of clients' financial information on a unified dashboard. In addition, users will be granted access to QuickBooks Online Advanced for the purpose of managing their financial records.

- The user did not provide any text to rewrite. QuickBooks Online Accountant offers the opportunity to enhance your visibility and attract potential clients by utilizing a distinctive Find-a-ProAdvisor profile, which is provided at no cost upon obtaining QuickBooks ProAdvisor certification. This feature facilitates the acquisition of desired leads for your services. The Intuit Marketing Hub provides a collection of templates and instructional materials aimed at enhancing brand development and converting potential leads into loyal consumers.

A warm and cordial greeting, certainly. Upon reviewing the aspects above, it can be inferred that the reader has acquired comprehensive knowledge regarding QuickBooks Online. The subsequent chapters will provide additional insights by delineating the many functionalities and capabilities

of both QuickBooks Online and QuickBooks Online Accountant (QBOA). It is advisable to record the acronyms as they will be employed in subsequent chapters, which will also feature activities that necessitate completion. It is advisable to allocate time for reading, studying, and engaging in regular practice.

Chapter 2: Visual Explanations and Guided Learning

QuickBooks Online ensures a highly engaging educational encounter suitable for individuals at all skill levels, including both novices and experienced users.

2.1 Addressing the Need for Visual Support

QuickBooks Online provides a collection of video tutorials for users who have a preference for visual aids. The comprehensive video tutorials provided encompass a diverse array of subjects, ranging from the first utilization of QuickBooks online to more intricate operations such as inventory management and payroll processing. The videos can be accessed through the help center, facilitating convenient learning and enabling users to follow the instructions effectively at their own pace.

Simplified Reporting

As an individual in a managerial position inside a commercial entity, it is incumbent upon you to fulfill the duty of disclosing essential financial information pertaining to your organization to prospective investors and other relevant parties with a vested interest. The utilization of graphical charts, representations, plus other visual aids within bookkeeping software facilitates the enhancement of data accuracy and the facilitation of effective communication, particularly in the context of attracting potential investors.

The individual in question bears the responsibility of effectively communicating with their subordinates, ensuring that they are informed on the financial condition of the organization. It is vital to ascertain the extent of the company's advancement and the manner in which individuals contribute to its overall growth. Bookkeeping accounting plays a crucial role in facilitating effective communication with one's team, fostering a sense of belonging and integration within the organization.

2.2 A Step-by-Step Guide to Using QuickBooks Online

Commencing one's journey with this widely-used accounting software need not be an intimidating endeavor. Below is a checklist that we have prepared for new individuals:

1. **Analyze and comprehend the functionality and features of your dashboard.**

There are two distinct configurations available for the QuickBooks dashboard. The perspective of a business or an accountant. For those occupying the role of a manager or business owner, it is often advantageous to adopt a business-oriented perspective. Conversely, accountants tend to focus on accounting-specific terminology and procedures when offering their viewpoint. The user can choose between the two options by selecting the Settings gear icon located in the upper right corner.

In due course, it is advisable to incorporate users into your arrangement. The principal administrator is typically designated as the main user. However, additional administrators or regular users can be incorporated, each with their specific degrees of access.

2. Include the relevant information regarding the company.

To access the desired menu, locate and click on the Settings gear icon positioned at the upper right corner of your dashboard. From the dropdown menu that appears, choose "Account and Settings" and proceed to select the "Company" option. The provided link directs users to a webpage containing their company details, where they can make modifications such as adding their company name, contact information, logo, and physical address, including both the legal and customer-facing addresses.

3. Establishing sales configurations

The "Account and Settings" menu encompasses the "Sales" and "Expenses" sections, which necessitate the input of data by novice users to facilitate accurate report generation inside the QuickBooks software.

Important features to incorporate in this context encompass the design and content of sales forms, the establishment of automated invoicing processes, the inclusion of value-added tax (VAT) particulars, and the specification of the year-end date for company reports. Various functions can be enabled or disabled, affording the user the ability to select which expenditures or sales components to utilize, ranging from buying orders to the monitoring of things based on the client.

4. Acquire business data

Users can transfer their pre-existing data spreadsheets into your QuickBooks system by accessing the Settings gear icon and opting for the "Import Data" option. Users can upload many types of files, including those that contain information on customers, products and services, suppliers, invoices, bills, sales receipts, credit notes, plus charts of accounts. Various file formats are accepted, including Microsoft Excel (MS Excel) and Comma-Separated Values (CSV) files.

5. Establish a connection between your bank cards.

Accounting software mostly revolves around establishing connections and incorporating crucial financial information such as debit cards, credit cards, and bank account details. To include your bank account, please navigate to the "Settings" section, followed by "Account and Settings," then proceed to "Bill Pay," and finally select "Bank Accounts."

6. Establish a connection between your payroll software.

QuickBooks Accounting facilitates the integration of external payroll systems while also providing its proprietary software solution. QuickBooks Payroll is regarded favorably and is prominently displayed as the "Payroll" tab on the user's dashboard.

Additionally, we can provide discounted offers on the most superior payroll software solution now available in the industry. Regardless of the specific service utilized, it is imperative to ensure its integration with the accounting software in order to streamline and automate the tax process.

7. Incorporate integrations

In addition, it is advisable to incorporate integrations with existing company software services. QuickBooks has a diverse array of connectors that encompass several domains, such as sales, marketing, compliance, and cash flow forecasting. To locate the desired resources, please access the QuickBooks App store.

8. Determine your tax requirements.

The onset of tax season is imminent for all individuals, necessitating proactive preparation on the part of businesses. Determine the applicable tax dates based on the state, federal, and local requirements that pertain to your business operations. If one utilizes QuickBooks Payroll, it possesses the requisite tax reporting capabilities to guide individuals through this procedure. However, it is important to note that federal and state identification numbers are still necessary.

QuickBooks Online Reconciliation

The term "reconciling" pertains to the significant accounting procedure of cross-verifying financial transactions with corresponding evidence in order to identify and rectify any inconsistencies.

How to reconcile a bank account?

The following instructions outline the process of utilizing QuickBooks software:

Step 1: Please provide a review or input the opening balance. Access the "Settings" option and navigate to the "Reconcile" tab inside the Tools section.

Step 2: Rectify any inconsistencies in the initial balance, if necessary. The initial sum you have may be satisfactory. However, in the event of a problem arising, it will be necessary for you to access the discrepancy report and make manual modifications to rectify the issue. QuickBooks can establish a connection between the user and the specified report.

Step 3: Please review the audit history. Certain differences arise due to the occurrence of many alterations, as opposed to a singular modification. In order to resolve this matter, it is necessary to navigate to the "View" option located under the history section. By doing so, the Audit History pertaining to the transaction inside question will be displayed. This feature enables users to view all modifications simultaneously.

Undoing Reconciliation in QuickBooks Online

In the event that a reconciliation process exhibits a significant number of inconsistencies, it may be advisable to consider the option of reversing said reconciliation. If there is a need to initiate a new beginning following a prior reconciliation, it is possible to request the assistance of an accountant that reverses the existing reconciliation.

In order to include your accountant in the system, it is imperative to devise a comprehensive design that accommodates multiple users. The following is a step-by-step procedure for incorporating an accountant into an organization:

To access the desired function, please navigate to the "Settings" tab, followed by the "Manage Users" option. From there, select the categories labeled "Accounting firms" and proceed to the "Invite" feature.

The accountant has the option to access the primary "Reconcile" page and proceed to select the "History by account" button located in the upper-right corner. This feature enables users to reverse the preceding transaction without the necessity of manually modifying each transaction within the register.

In addition, it is possible to manually modify each transaction.

1. Please access the Accounting section of the software, followed by selecting the option for Your Company. From there, proceed to the Chart of Accounts.

2. Please pick your account and go to the option of viewing the register.

3. Continuously choose the "R" status until it becomes blank or displays the letter "C" indicating clearance.

4. Click the "Save" button and choose the option "Yes" when requested to confirm.

Deleting a Deposit in QuickBooks

Occasionally, it may be necessary to remove deposits. It is possible that the entry was made erroneously or that a duplicate of a valid deposit was included. In order to remove a deposit in QuickBooks Online, it is necessary to follow the following procedures:

1. Please access the Settings menu and proceed to the Banking section. From there, select the option to Make Deposits.

2. In the event that the Payments to the Deposit box become accessible, it is advised to choose the option "Cancel."

3. To navigate through the existing transactions and locate the deposit that you intend to remove, please select the "Previous" option.

4. To initiate the deletion of a deposit, please navigate to the "Edit" menu and select the "Delete Deposit" option.

Tips to use QuickBooks Online

1. After acquiring proficiency in utilizing the QuickBooks Online accounting software in daily operations, it is advisable to incorporate additional strategies and techniques to optimize the overall user experience.

2. Establishing recurring invoicing is a crucial aspect of efficient financial management in various organizational settings. The concept of "set-it-and-forget-it" encapsulates the prevailing approach.

3. It is advisable to consider incorporating a spellcheck feature. The spellcheck feature in QuickBooks can be activated or deactivated by accessing the program's settings with the following steps: Edit > Preferences > Speller.

4. It is advisable to consistently and frequently save one's work. The act of preserving any given form can be accomplished by pressing the key combination Alt + S (or Option + Control + S for users of Mac operating systems).

5. It is advisable to engage in the practice of reconciling one's bank, savings, and credit card accounts on a monthly basis. Maintaining vigilance over the process will guarantee its continued simplicity.

6. Keyboard shortcuts can be utilized to enhance efficiency in various tasks, not limited to saving operations.

7. Please ensure that you attach a receipt to each of your expense entries. This practice establishes a documented record that can serve as evidence to support your reimbursement claims.

8. The transition from physical payments to electronic payments: It is advisable, if feasible, to discontinue the practice of issuing physical checks for business expenditures, as digital payment methods offer greater ease of automation.

How to create an invoice?

There are two methods available for generating an invoice in QuickBooks: the creation of a new invoice from the beginning or the generation of an invoice based on an existing estimate.

From Scratch in QuickBooks Online:

Step 1: Go To 'Invoice'

To initiate the creation of an invoice in QuickBooks Online, users should navigate to the top of your left menu bar on their dashboard and click on the "+ New" button. Subsequently, they should proceed to select "Invoice" from the first column located under the "Customers" section.

Step 2: Add New Invoice Information

Please furnish the requisite details from your invoice screen in order to finalize your invoice.

Step 3: Save & Send the Invoice

To delay the transmission of the invoice after ensuring its accuracy, users should select the Save option located in the lower right corner of the screen. To preview or print the invoice prior to saving or sending it, users can click on the Print or Preview button located at the bottom menu bar of their invoice screen. Following this, they should proceed to select the Print or Preview option from the drop-down menu.

Upon selecting the Print or Preview option, users will be able to visualize the appearance of their invoice.

To expedite the transmission of your invoice, use the option "Save & Send." The QuickBooks software can generate an email automatically, utilizing the predefined settings that have been established. If desired, it is possible to personalize a default email message associated with this invoice. To transmit the email, please click on the green button labeled "Send and close." Subsequently, a notification will be issued to inform you that the invoice has been successfully transmitted to your customer via email.

Convert an Estimate to an Invoice in QuickBooks Online:

Step 1: Go to Estimates

To access the Estimates section, please navigate to the Sales tab on your left menu bar and hover over it. From the dropdown menu, select the option labeled Estimates. In the previous iteration of QuickBooks, an Estimates drop-down menu was absent, necessitating the user to manually travel to the Customers section.

Step 2: Locate the Estimate

The Estimates page provides a comprehensive list of all pending estimates.

To see the details of your estimate, click on any part of your estimate entry line. Upon initiation, a novel pop-up window shall manifest, presenting pivotal details pertaining to your estimate, encompassing the sum, date of transaction, and estimate-related activities. To initiate modifications, please locate and select the green Edit button situated at the lower right corner of the window. In addition, it is possible to execute further actions, such as replicating the estimation.

Step 3: Convert that Estimate into an Invoice

To initiate the process of generating an invoice, kindly locate and select the "Create invoice" option situated on the rightmost section of your estimate entry interface.

Subsequently, a pop-up window will be displayed, prompting the user to specify the specific portion of your estimate that they intend to invoice. The user has the option to convert either the complete estimate or a partial section of the invoice. This practice proves to be advantageous in facilitating progress billing for larger-scale projects. Next, proceed to select the "Create invoice" button.

Upon selecting the Create invoice button, QuickBooks Online shows the display of the create invoice screen, wherein all the fields will be automatically supplied with the relevant information derived from the estimate data. Subsequently, you have the opportunity to thoroughly examine and implement any modifications that you deem necessary.

Step 4: Press Save or Save & Send

After supplying all the necessary information and confirming your contentment with the invoice, proceed to select the option of either saving or saving and sending it. To promptly dispatch the invoice, opt for the "Save and Send" option and proceed in the same manner as outlined in the previous step of the invoice creation process from its inception.

Chapter 3: Creating a QuickBooks Online Company

After accessing QuickBooks Online, users are immediately prompted to create their own company. The initial step involves the inclusion of essential data either by starting from the beginning, importing data from QuickBooks Desktop if applicable, or importing lists such as customers, vendors, and inventory items.

3.1 QuickBooks Online Sign-up

The decision has been made to employ QuickBooks as the financial management software for your organization. A fundamental principle to adhere to when utilizing QuickBooks Online is to ensure that the activities recorded in the software accurately reflect real-world transactions and events. All transactions, encompassing activities such as sales tracking and bank deposits, are encompassed within this category. Although certain tasks, like as invoice submission, are exclusively performed within QuickBooks, the majority of recorded activities are often executed in external contexts.

It is imperative to ensure that the accounting process effectively and precisely records every phase of each transaction, encompassing credit card payments, staff remuneration facilitated through QuickBooks Payroll and acquisition of loans from financial institutions. It involves conducting a comparison between the documented transactions on one's authentic bank statements and the corresponding details such as names, dates, payment methods, and amounts.

- To commence, please navigate to the website quickbooks.intuit.com/pricing.

- The user's text is too brief to be rewritten academically. Please search four categories that delineate the Simple Start, Plus, Essentials, and Advanced subscription plans. To access QuickBooks Self-Employed, navigate to the section dedicated to freelancers and independent contractors located below the provided boxes. Users are presented with the option to select either a 30-day complimentary trial or three months with discounted rates for the Simple Start, Plus, and Essentials plans. It is important to mention that the Advanced membership does not include a complimentary trial. However, users have the option to access the drive by visiting qbo.intuit.com/redir/testdrive_us_advanced.

- The user's text does not contain any information to rewrite academically. To initiate a complimentary trial, kindly select the slider button located at the upper section of the QuickBooks edition. This action will launch the 30-day free trial period. It should be noted that opting to make an immediate purchase of the software will result in greater savings and a reduced subscription cost, as discounts are not applicable to free trial versions. It is important to note that promotional pricing often concludes after three months.

3.2 Company's contact info

To input contact information for QuickBooks plus your clients, click within the Contact info box, which includes the pencil symbol.

Company Phone: Please provide the telephone number that must be displayed on the sales documents received by consumers.

Email: The designated email address utilized by QuickBooks for communication with the administrator corresponds to the business email associated with the user. The customer-facing email address will be included in the sales forms of your clients, such as invoices. Please deselect the option and provide the appropriate address if it differs from the email address of the QuickBooks administrator.

Website: To ensure its inclusion on all sales forms, please provide a website address.

3.3 Investigating your new Company

Companies inside QuickBooks Online exhibit similar characteristics to conventional companies in the external business environment. Below are many of these characteristics:

- Access to the company's dashboard can be obtained by logging onto the QuickBooks account.

- The Account and Settings feature may be accessed by clicking on the gear button. To proceed, select the Company tab inside the Account and Settings section.

1. **Company Name**

- To make alterations to the information pertaining to the company's name, one must click on any part of the business name section, including the representation of a pencil.

- The user's text does not contain any information to rewrite academically. Please ensure to click the "Save" button once you have made the required modifications.

The firm name section enumerates three components:

Legal and Company name: Please provide the precise format in which you would like your company name to be shown on invoices and forms. The name registered with the Internal Revenue Service (IRS) for your firm must align with the official business name. In tax-related documentation, such as payroll tax returns and form 1099, the individual's legal name will be employed. Please deselect the checkbox and provide your legal name in the event that it is distinct from the desired firm name to be displayed on your invoices.

EIN: The Employer Identification Number (EIN) provided to you should align with this. If an individual is self-employed, they may utilize their Social Security number. Due to the confidential nature of EINs, QuickBooks may require users to authenticate their log in credentials prior to accessing or modifying the EIN.

Company Logo: Please import the official logo of your company in order to incorporate it into the forms you're going to generate. It is important to save the logo onto a computer system in the form of an image file. To incorporate your brand into QuickBooks Online, follow these prescribed steps;

- It is recommended that the user selects the gray square located adjacent to the company logo.

- The logos that have been previously submitted to QuickBooks Online are displayed on the subsequent screen. If the emblem is already present, it is advisable to incorporate it inside the compilation of the company's particulars. Please select the blue plus symbol if the desired logo is not currently displayed.

- QuickBooks provides a pop-up window that enables users to navigate their computer's file system and select the desired logo image file.

- To return to the previous screen and view a miniature representation of your newly selected logo, please click on the "Open" button. The logo is stored within your QuickBooks Online account, eliminating the need for manual refreshing when customizing forms.

- Please ensure that you have selected the logo you like to add by highlighting it, and then proceed to click on the Save button.

Type of Company: To submit or amend the information regarding your company type, users can click on the pencil icon or other designated spot within the Company Type section.

Please select the appropriate taxable entity type by clicking on the drop-down menu located next to the Tax form box.

- **Partnership:** Opt for this business category if two or more partners operate your firm. Partnerships utilize Form 1065 as a means to disclose the financial gains and losses of their company operations.

- **A C corporation:** A C-corp is a type of corporate entity that is subject to separate taxation from its owners, as opposed to the pass-through taxation structure. C-corporations file their reports using Form 1120.

- **LLC:** A limited liability company is a legal business entity that provides its owners with limited liability protection. When faced with uncertainty over the appropriate tax filing status, namely whether to classify oneself as a sole owner, a partnership, or an S-corporation, it is advisable to choose this particular corporate form.

- **Sole Proprietorship:** In the context of business operations, a sole proprietorship refers to a business structure wherein an individual assumes full responsibility and control over all aspects of the enterprise. The income or losses should be reported using Schedule C, which is a component of Form 1040.

- **S corporation**: S-corp is a type of corporation that elects to be treated as such for tax purposes. This classification requires the organization to file Form 1120S, which allows for the distribution of corporate revenue, loss, and taxes to its shareholders.

- **A nonprofit organization,** Often known as a tax-exempt entity, is a type of corporation that places a higher emphasis on achieving social objectives rather than maximizing financial gains. The disclosure of their annual activities is made through the submission of Form 990.

2. Company Address

To update or edit the address information of your organization, please select the pencil icon or other designated spot within the address section. In this particular edition of QuickBooks Online, the corporate address, customer-facing address, and legal address are each presented as distinct entities.

Customer-facing address: The address indicated on invoices plus other sales documents serves as the designated location to which clients are advised to remit their money. Please deselect the checkbox and provide the appropriate customer-facing address if it is different from your corporate address.

- To save any edits made, please click on the "Save" button.

Company address: The company address refers to the physical location of the organization and is utilized for the purpose of remitting payments to QuickBooks.

- Please remember to click the "Save" button once you have made the required modifications.

Legal/Official Address: Your tax filings must be submitted to the official address, which must align with the address you have registered with the Internal Revenue Service (IRS). Once more, it is necessary to deselect the option and furnish the legal address if it differs from the address of the company.

- Please click the "Save" button in the color green if you are satisfied with the address you have mentioned.

3.4 Inactivating or editing accounts

Ensure that your chart of accounts is organized and devoid of unnecessary complexity. One can render an account inactive if there is no intention to utilize it further. For the aim of facilitating reporting activities, QuickBooks opts to render accounts inactive instead of permanently eradicating them, thereby granting users access to previous transaction data.

An account can be expeditiously rendered inactive in cases where it has never been utilized or when the balance remaining is zero dollars. However, active accounts will necessitate further exertion. The removal of data from a single account has a consequential effect on the other accounts due to the interdependence of balanced accounts.

Key considerations to be aware of before deactivating an account:

- With the exception of merging two accounts, it is not feasible to permanently remove an account.

- Transactions conducted on an account that is deemed inactive persist within the account. Transactions involving deactivated (removed) accounts are unaffected.

- It is not possible to make edits to a transaction that is associated with an inactive account. In order to effectively modify or remove the transaction, it is necessary to initiate the restoration process for the account. Subsequently, proceed to the register and proceed with the removal of each discrete entry. Prior to deactivating the account, it is imperative to thoroughly assess and rectify any outstanding amount associated with it.

- It is imperative to ensure that the balance is adjusted to zero prior to classifying an account as inactive on your balance sheet. In the event that the balance is non-zero, QuickBooks Online will generate an adjustment entry in order to reconcile the balance of the inactive account to zero. The automated entry is indistinguishable from posting to previous years as it is allocated towards the Opening Balance Equity account. The submission may lead to the submission of erroneous tax data.

Making an account inactive

When an account with a remaining balance is deactivated, QuickBooks automatically generates a journal entry. Consequently, the leftover balance is then moved to an alternative account. The financial records retain the existing transactions and do not disappear. Nevertheless, QuickBooks does not automatically update the journal item or readjust the balance if the account is reused.

There are specific procedures that must be followed in order to deactivate certain accounts:

- Modify the associated account for the utilization of products or services, if applicable. In an alternative approach, it is possible to turn off any services or products that are associated with the account.

- To eliminate an income account with pending charges, it is advisable to issue invoices to your clients for the time, billable costs, or charges incurred. Subsequently, the account has the potential to be eliminated.

- It is imperative to dissociate any recurring transactions that are associated with an account.

- If an account in the chart of accounts has subaccounts, it is advisable to relocate these subaccounts to a distinct account. It is not possible to delete subaccounts that contain accounts.

At present, it appears that all necessary components are in place, and the procedure is nearing its conclusion. To finalize the inactivation process, please adhere to the following steps:

- To access the Charts of Accounts, please navigate to the Settings menu and select the option labeled "Charts of Accounts."

- Identify the specific account that you intend to remove.

- To initiate the desired action, the user should navigate to the Action dropdown menu and subsequently select the Make inactive option.

Dormant accounts and their corresponding transactions will remain observable upon generating reports. The inclusion of QuickBooks serves to uphold precision. Certain reports can be tailored in order to conceal inactive accounts. Nevertheless, it is important to note that implementing such customization may result in a decrease in the overall accuracy of those reports.

To get information regarding your dormant accounts, please adhere to the following instructions:

- To access the Chart of Accounts, please navigate to the Settings tab and select the option labeled "Chart of Accounts."

- Adjacent to the printer symbol, select the Settings icon.

- Select the checkbox labeled "Include inactive."

3.5 Updating the Chart of Accounts

The chart of accounts provides a comprehensive compilation of all the accounts employed by QuickBooks for the purpose of organizing and managing financial data. These accounts serve the purpose of categorizing transactions across many types of documents, such as reports, tax forms, and sales forms. Each account possesses a transaction history that provides a comprehensive record of the financial activities, including the balance of funds held and the amount of outstanding debt.

The chart of accounts holds a pivotal role in maintaining robust accounting practices, so it is imperative to have a comprehensive understanding of its structure and ensure its accurate implementation.

- To access and analyze your chart of accounts, navigate to the Settings menu and select "Chart of Accounts."

The organization of accounts is facilitated through the utilization of column type, name, and detail type. The content displayed on significant financial reports, such as the Profit and loss statements and Balance Sheet, is contingent upon the types of accounts and levels of detail involved.

The examination of current balance and transaction history can be conducted through the perusal of account histories across many accounts. It is possible to generate a report that provides an overview of transactions associated with accounts lacking a transactional history.

- To access the historical records or generate reports pertaining to the chart of accounts list, you may choose either the "Account history" or "Run a report" options available in the Action column.

3.6 Adding account numbers

As your company grows, the range of accounts utilized for financial classification also develops. There is no need for concern if the chart of accounts you are using is extensive in size. Through the process of assigning numerical values, one is able to maintain a well-structured and easily accessible system for organizing and locating various accounts.

The account numbers option is turned off by default. The following instructions outline the process for activating it:

- To begin, navigate to the Settings menu and proceed to select the Account and settings option.

- Select the option labeled "Advanced" within the tab.

- To initiate the editing process, please navigate to the "Chart of Accounts" section and locate the "Edit" option.

- Please activate the feature to enable account numbers. To enable the display of account numbers on transactions and reports, select the option "Show account numbers."

- To complete the task, please click on the "Save" button followed by the "Done" button.

Once the account numbers have been activated, please proceed to follow the subsequent instructions in order to utilize this feature:

- To access the Chart of Accounts, please navigate to the Bookkeeping section and click on the corresponding option.

- To initiate the batch editing process, please select the "Batch edit" option found at the top of the Action column.

- Please include the account numbers within the designated Number column.

- After following the procedures above, proceed to click on the Save button.

The process of locating certain accounts within the Chart of Accounts or inputting transactions has been optimized to reduce time consumption. Employ the numerical values provided to efficiently find the respective accounts.

3.7 Importing a chart of accounts

The chart of accounts serves as a tool within QuickBooks for the purpose of systematically organizing all accounting-related activities. The chart of accounts in QuickBooks is customized to suit the specific needs of your organization during the initial setup process. Users have the option to import their pre-existing accounts from another QuickBooks Online or Desktop company file or a spreadsheet containing bespoke accounts. It allows for the avoidance of manual entry of all account information.

 To import your chart of accounts, it is necessary to prepare your spreadsheet, upload it, and map the fields in your spreadsheet to the corresponding fields in QuickBooks. It may be done using Excel, Google Sheets, or CSV files. Once these steps are completed, you can proceed with importing your chart of accounts. We will guide you through each of the steps above.

Upload spreadsheet

- To access QuickBooks Online, please proceed with the sign-in process.

- To initiate the process, navigate to the "Settings" tab and proceed to select the "Import Data" option.

- The task at hand involves the selection of a Chart of Accounts.

- To initiate the process of uploading a file from the computer, you need to click on the "Browse" option. Subsequently, you will be prompted to select the desired file for upload, after which you should click on "Open."

- Alternatively, if you like to upload data from Google Sheets, you may opt to Connect and sign in to your Google account. Please select the appropriate file.

- Please proceed by selecting the "Next" option.

Formatting spreadsheet

- To commence, either access an extant account spreadsheet or initiate a novel one. In an alternative approach, it is possible to import the chart of accounts from a distinct QuickBooks firm.

- It is imperative to include specific columns in your spreadsheet, including Account Type, name, Detail Type, and Number.

- If one is arranging their accounts based on numerical order, it is advisable to include a column for the account numbers. If account numbers are not utilized, this step can be skipped.

- When incorporating a sub-account, adhere to the subsequent format inside the Account Name column: The sub-account serves as the principal account. The topic of discussion is the utility of gas, serving as an illustrative example.

- It is advisable to store your spreadsheet in either Excel, Google Sheets, or CSV format, provided that all the data appears to be accurate and complete.

Import your chart of accounts.

- Please review the settings provided above to ensure that all tasks have been completed accurately.

- The user's text does not contain any information to rewrite. In the event that a particular field is visually emphasized through the use of the color red, it is advisable to position the cursor over said area in order to reveal any necessary corrections or adjustments that may be required.

- Any account that the user does not desire to retain can be deselected.

- Choose the "Import" option if all aspects are satisfactory.

Mapping spreadsheet fields to QuickBooks fields

- After the successful upload of your spreadsheet, proceed to establish the necessary mappings for your accounts to ensure their smooth importation.

- To complete the task, navigate to the Your Field column and select the little arrow icon. Proceed to align the names with the corresponding QuickBooks Online fields for Detail Type, Account name, Type, and Account number.

- If there is a discrepancy between a field and a column in the spreadsheet, excluding the Account Name, you have the option to select "No Match." For instance, if account numbers are not utilized.

- Please select the "Next" button.

3.8 Company preferences

Usage statistics

Usage limits in QuickBooks pertain to the maximum number of accounts or users that can be concurrently active. The user is subject to a use limit that is determined by their subscription. The limitations imposed on QuickBooks pertain to the inclusion of charts of accounts, billable users, classes, tags, and locations.

The implementation of a subscription model in QuickBooks Online results in alterations to the limitations on usage. The limitation is exclusively applicable to persons who are actively engaged or have been invited, as well as to accounts, classes, places, and tags.

The quantity of items allocated for each consumption threshold is presented on the usage limits dashboard. In order to see the latest usage limits, accountants are advised to log in directly to their clients' accounts.

- To access QuickBooks Online with administrative privileges, please proceed to sign in.

- To begin, navigate to the "Settings" option and proceed to select "Account and settings."

- Please navigate to the Usage tab.

There is no need for concern in the event that the user reaches the maximum limit of their usage capacity and becomes unable to include more users or accounts. There are two potential courses of action available: either upgrading one's subscription level or reducing one's use. It is vital to evaluate the utilization of resources for each company in the event of managing many entities.

Sales preferences

Under the Sales tab, users can establish payment terms, customize sales forms to suit their preferences, and exercise control over the information displayed on customer forms. Moreover, this is the point at which you activate features such as automated reminders and incremental invoicing.

3.9 Customizing sales forms

QuickBooks Online offers the capability to generate visually appealing estimates, professional invoices, and sales receipts.

Modifying the visual appearance and aesthetic qualities of sales forms is a convenient and efficient method for enhancing internal communication inside an organization. The ability to construct aesthetically pleasing forms does not necessitate expertise in design. Moreover, you are afforded the opportunity to use discretion in curating the material that your clientele peruses, selectively incorporating solely the indispensable elements pertinent to your organization.

Users can create and personalize templates for sales estimates, receipts, and invoices. This document offers guidance on the process of modifying sales forms.

Create a new template.

- To begin, navigate to the settings menu and select the option labeled "Custom form styles."
- Please select a new style.
- Please select a specific sales form type for which you would want to develop a template.

Tailor the visual presentation

- Please select the Design tab.
- Please assign a name to your template.
- To select your desired layout, please click on the option labeled "Change up the template." It should be noted that the layouts in question are of a set nature.

- One may opt to engage in logo editing for the purpose of making necessary modifications to their logo or concealing it entirely.

- To modify the logo, please click on the addition icon (+) located on the image. Please select a logo from your existing collection or input a new logo. Only one logo can be utilized simultaneously, although it is possible to store many logos.

- To modify the dimensions and positioning of the logo, please choose the appropriate icons for size adjustment and placement manipulation.

- Click on the Hide logo option in order to obscure the logo.

- The user is requesting to select an option from a button or image. Experiment with alternative colors and explore other shades. To obtain a distinct color, one can utilize a HEX code, which is a six-digit alphanumeric combination representing a specific hue.

- To modify the font size, please click on the option labeled "Select a different font."

- To modify the margins, use the option "Edit print settings." Ensuring the transmission of printed forms to clients is of utmost importance.

Customizing the info on your forms

- Select the Content tab.

- The user's text does not contain any information to rewrite. To initiate the modification of a specific area, the user should select the table, header, or footer within the provided form as a starting point. Each section must be edited separately.

- The user's text lacks sufficient information to be rewritten academically. The user can selectively exhibit designated fields on their form by marking the corresponding checkboxes. Next, in order to modify the provided template, select a different component, such as the header, table, or footer.

- Once the necessary modifications have been made, please proceed by selecting the "Done" option.

3.10 Reviewing Company Settings

The user can access and make changes to their firm's name, address, contact details, and Employer Identification Number (EIN) through the Company tab. Furthermore, users have the option to make adjustments to their Intuit marketing settings.

3.11 Additional preferences

Payment preferences

Users have the option to establish a connection between an already existing QuickBooks Payments account and QuickBooks Online by accessing the Payments tab. Alternatively; they can choose to configure online payment settings inside the same platform. Upon establishing a connection, users are granted the ability to manage merchant information and business owner data, as well as designate the specific location inside QuickBooks for automated deposit recording.

Advanced preferences

Additional functionality in QuickBooks can be enabled by accessing the Advanced tab. Not all individuals are consistently activated. One example of the functionality is the ability to activate categories for the purpose of systematically monitoring and organizing goods and services. The commencement and conclusion of the fiscal year for your organization are also determined at this location. This option can be enabled in this location if your business engages in transactions involving multiple currencies.

Expenses preferences

Users have the option to activate billable charges and buy orders on the charges page. Additionally, they can customize the email notifications associated with purchase orders.

Time preferences

The Time tab provides users with the ability to establish the commencement of the workweek, track the services rendered by their team during client engagements, and decide whether or not to disclose the pricing details of these services to staff members and vendors.

BOOK TWO

FOCUS AND ACCOUNTING

Chapter 4: A Focus on Bookkeeping and Accounting

The discipline of bookkeeping is primarily concerned with the administration of financial records through the systematic documentation of transactions, the oversight of accounts, and the meticulous recording of pertinent financial information.

4.1 Navigating QuickBooks Online for Your Business

Efficiently navigating through an application is crucial for optimizing productivity. Effective navigation plays a pivotal role in facilitating a seamless and pleasurable user experience, whereas a subpar navigation system can engender frustration and result in errors. Fortunately, QuickBooks Online boasts a thoroughly tested navigation system that facilitates reasonable access to all necessary features and functionalities.

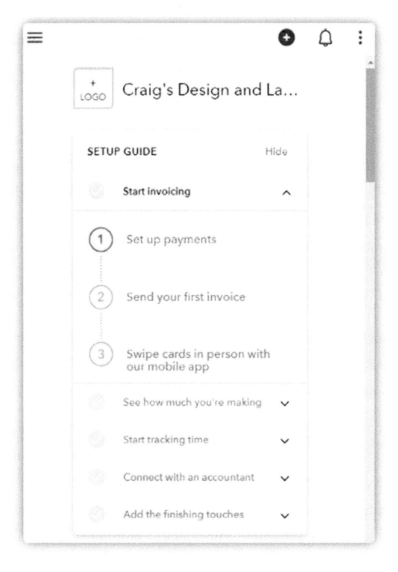

The responsiveness of QuickBooks Online's user interface is a significant factor to consider. It implies that the arrangement of elements is responsive and adapts to the varying screen widths. In the event that the website is accessed via a smartphone with a limited screen width, the layout will diverge from that observed on a computer with a broader screen. Although the arrangement may undergo alterations, the substantive information included inside the pages will remain unchanged. One can observe the visual representation of QuickBooks Online on a mobile device by adjusting the width of the browser window on a PC.

It is presumed that the user is accessing QuickBooks Online using a web browser on their personal computer. Upon arrival at the landing page, it becomes evident that there exist two distinct and opposing sections. The left section of the interface features a black backdrop and is referred to as the Navigation Pane. The primary section of the interface, characterized by a white background, is known as the Dashboard.

We will examine the Dashboard first. It is important to note that Intuit undergoes periodic reorganizations of its user interface, which may result in minor variations in the layout upon viewing.

The Header

The Header refers to the narrow and unchanging section located at the uppermost part of the screen. It is characterized by three horizontal bars positioned on the left side, while a collection of icons is situated on the right side. Located at the uppermost section of the primary window region, one will see the designation of the organization adjacent to a set of three horizontal lines.

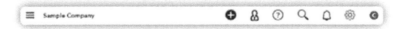

Upon selecting the horizontal bars, it becomes evident that the Navigation Pane located on the left-hand side becomes concealed. Upon subsequent activation, the item resurfaces. To access the Navigation Pane on a mobile device, it is necessary to tap on the three bars icon.

It is worth noting that the presence of the Navigation Pane in a hidden state triggers the appearance of a '+' button at the upper section of the Dashboard. This button serves as a replacement for the New button, which was originally located within the Navigation Pane. The buttons possess the same functionality. These entities are employed to include various additions to an organization, encompassing clientele, suppliers, personnel, and financial institutions.

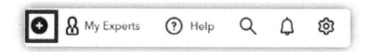

The subsequent symbol displayed on the Heading bears a resemblance to a human being and serves the purpose of accessing the feature known as "My Experts." It is the location where users can authorize their accountants to access their QuickBooks Online account. Additionally, QuickBooks has the functionality to search for a certified accountant located within your geographical vicinity.

Following the My Experts button, there currently is a supplementary button labeled "help." Users can input an inquiry, which will then lead them to a suggested response from the community site. Users have the option to directly inquire with QuickBooks Online's support team by selecting the "Contact Us" option located at the bottom of the interface.

The subsequent icon located within the Header window is the Search icon, visually, such as a magnifying glass. It pertains to the process of searching within the organizational file repository. Various types of information can be searched for, such as the name or location of a client or vendor, specific transactions, certain monetary amounts, or transactions that occurred on a particular day. Additionally, users have the option to utilize the Advanced Search feature, which aids in the process of refining search parameters to effectively limit desired results.

Subsequently, the user will encounter the Notifications icon that bears a resemblance to a bell. It is the location where users can access new alerts. Notifications can be received for many events, including the receipt of a new bill or the payment of an invoice by a customer.

The Settings symbol represents the subsequent element within the Header pane. The object exhibits a gear-like form. Upon clicking this button, a window will be opened, providing access to a variety of settings that can be adjusted according to the user's preferences. The primary classifications encompassed under this context are Company, Tools, Lists, and Profile.

- Company

In the settings section pertaining to the Company category, users can modify their Accounts and Settings. This area encompasses various pieces of information, including but not limited to the business type, company address, and tax number. Users can access the "Manage Users" feature to establish user profiles for QuickBooks Online. This functionality allows users to define the privileges and permissions associated with each profile within the application. Users can personalize the appearance of forms by modifying color schemes and incorporating their logos. Additionally, one may navigate to the Chart of Accounts in order to assess the financial position of the organization. Users have the option to explore novel and experimental plug-ins in QuickBooks by accessing QuickBooks Labs.

- Tools

Additionally, there exists a multitude of utilities that can be readily accessed through this specific menu item. Users can engage in various actions within the system, such as placing orders for checks, importing and exporting data, as well as reconciling data to ensure its consistency. In addition, there exist many features that facilitate the creation of a budget, enable the auditing of QuickBooks Online usage by individual users, allow the sharing of a SmartLook code via a QuickBooks Online expert to facilitate screen sharing during support calls, and provide a Case Center for the submission of document requests.

- Lists

Lists provide a comprehensive overview of valuable information pertaining to your organization. The components above encompass a comprehensive compilation of your merchandise, recurring transactions, and approved modes of payment, stipulations pertaining to payment deadlines and reductions, as well as the ability to append file attachments to transactions.

- Profile

The final category inside the options menu is denoted as Profile. On this platform, users can provide feedback, which may encompass the option of uploading screenshots or files. The data privacy policies of QuickBooks Online can also be accessed for viewing.

Moreover, the settings screen provides the option to alternate between Accountant View and Business View for your viewing preferences. The act of switching between views does not result in any alteration of the underlying data. The Business View feature caters to individuals who possess limited familiarity with accounting principles, whereas the Accounting View option is designed to accommodate seasoned accountants who are well-versed in the subject matter and employ more specialized language. The Cash Flow chart, a feature exclusively accessible through QuickBooks Labs when in Accountant mode, is encompassed within the Business mode. The arrangement of Navigation Pane items also exhibits modest variations across different views.

The final element within this stationary panel is a graphical representation denoting the user's Intuit account. By clicking on this link, users will be able to amend their account information and initiate the sign-out process.

The help, search, and settings icons may return on many screens within the QuickBooks Online interface. In such instances, it is imperative to exercise caution and discernment in selecting the appropriate option. The icons present in this context will be designated as being located within the Header section.

Navigation Pane

The navigation pane is situated on the left side of your screen and is characterized by its vertical orientation. The current region lacks the capability for scrolling. The user can activate or deactivate the feature by selecting the menu icon located within the Heading.

The primary elements of the Navigation Pane consist of a New button and multiple rollover menu items. By placing the cursor above a menu item accompanied by an arrow, further menu options will be displayed.

The inclusion of the New button provides users with reasonable access to the creation of many types of business papers. The entities above are classified into four distinct categories, namely Customers, Employees, Vendors, and Others. In subsequent lectures, we will delve further into the diverse functions that are enumerated in this document.

Clicking on the subsequent element within the Navigation Pane will direct the user to your Dashboard screen. The Dashboard view is set as the default when logging in. However, selecting this option while in any additional view will redirect the user back to the primary Dashboard window.

The subsequent option on the menu pertains to the field of banking. From this platform, users are able to securely access and view all of their associated credit card and banking transactions. Categorization of transactions is a valuable practice that facilitates a comprehensive understanding of the purpose and nature of each transaction.

The subsequent element pertains to expenditures. It is the platform where one may observe the financial outflows from their business operations. Additionally, it is possible to effectively oversee and coordinate all the merchants that necessitate payment.

Sales follow expenses in the financial statement. The invoicing function is situated within this designated area, serving as the central hub for configuring the various payment methods employed by your organization. This platform facilitates the establishment of client profiles and the display of products and services offered by the business.

Within the realm of project management, it is possible to monitor and analyze the financial aspects of individual projects, specifically focusing on the profits generated and expenses incurred. This feature can be accessed exclusively by subscribers of QuickBooks Online Plus or QuickBooks Online Advanced.

The subsequent option on the menu is Payroll. This platform facilitates the management of both workers and contractors. One can reimburse their employees and ensure adherence to workers' compensation regulations.

The Reports section of QuickBooks Online provides users with access to a wide range of comprehensive reporting functionalities. Users have the option to select from pre-existing standard reports or create their customized reports.

The Taxes menu option provides users with the ability to configure their sales tax settings. Users can document their tax payments and access tax reports.

The Mileage menu option allows users to effectively monitor and record the distance traveled during driving activities. The monitoring of this can be accomplished either through the utilization of a mobile application or by manually inputting the distance in miles.

The subsequent item on the menu pertains to the field of Accounting. The Chart of Accounts is available for viewing, providing a comprehensive overview of the financial aspects pertaining to your firm. Additionally, one might engage in the practice of reconciling accounts, whereby the objective is to maintain congruity between one's internal financial records and the corresponding bank statements.

The subsequent item on the menu is labeled "My Accountant." An accountant can be included in the team by extending an invitation via electronic mail. In the event that an individual does not possess an accountant, QuickBooks Online's directory can be utilized as a resource to facilitate the identification of a suitable professional.

The final item on the menu pertains to insurance. Comprehensive information pertaining to many insurance categories, such as automobile, cyber security, and workers' compensation, can be obtained to address the insurance requirements of your firm.

The Dashboard

Positioned beneath the Header and situated adjacent to the Navigation Pane, the major part of the Dashboard is characterized by its scrollable nature. The Dashboard provides a comprehensive summary of key aspects pertaining to your business, encompassing cash flow, expenses, invoices, sales, and profit and loss. Furthermore, access to information pertaining to bank accounts becomes available subsequent to their successful linkage.

Adjacent to a prominently displayed button for logo insertion, the company's name will be rendered in a sizeable typeface. Located on the extreme right side of the corporate denomination is a toggle button used to control privacy settings. Activating the Privacy toggle leads to the concealment of all data displayed on the dashboard. This feature can prove advantageous in situations where an unauthorized individual gains proximity to your workstation and should not be privy to such information.

The Setup Guide can be found below the company name. The concealment of this particular region can be achieved by utilizing the Hide button located on the right-hand side. In the following section, we shall examine this guide, notwithstanding the fact that all the information included within is readily available in other sections of the application.

The Setup Guide

The initial component outlined in the Setup Guide pertains to the process of invoicing. Users will have the capability to establish payment arrangements, initiate their initial invoice, and conduct in-person card transactions upon enrollment in the corresponding service.

In the subsequent section of the Setup Guide, users will have the opportunity to ascertain their earnings. This area provides the functionality to establish a connection with your financial institution. Users can review their transactions and analyze their profits within this platform.

One alternative is to initiate the practice of monitoring and recording the passage of time. Clicking on this will direct you to a webpage where you can proceed with the enrollment process for TSheets. TSheets operates independently from QuickBooks. However, it does offer a complimentary trial period.

The fourth alternative presented in the Setup Guide entails establishing a connection with an accountant. Within this particular segment, it is possible to extend an invitation to an accountant for the purpose of seeing your company's data by inputting their email address. Additionally, a hyperlink is provided herein to access a directory that facilitates the search for certified accountants in close proximity to your current location.

The last alternative is to apply the concluding details. Within this particular section, individuals have the opportunity to refine and enhance their profile, facilitate the acceptance of online payments by consenting to the Merchant Agreement, and establish sales tax information.

The order in which the remaining window regions on the main screen are displayed may vary based on the width of your browser window being used. When the screen width is minimized, such as when accessing the content from a smartphone, the initial area that appears is the Bank Accounts window.

Bank accounts will display a comprehensive record of dual-entry accounting (both credit and debit accounts) that have been inputted. If the accounts are connected to the user's bank, they will have access to the most recent transaction information. If not, it will be necessary to manually update transactions. Users can access their transaction history for each account by selecting the respective account from the provided list.

The subsequent window that appears is the Invoices window. It illustrates the recorded amounts owed to a business entity by its customers for goods or services provided on credit. The presentation of unpaid funds takes precedence over that of paid funds.

Following the Invoices pane comes the Expenses window. It pertains to the accounts payable function. The bills above encompass those that you have inputted.

The subsequent display exhibits a concise overview of your financial gains and losses. The income is displayed in conjunction with the expenses, accompanied by the corresponding count of transactions to be reviewed for each category.

The final panel is designated for sales. The user will be presented with a line chart, whereby each data point can be selected to access a corresponding report.

Furthermore, when operating in the Business View as opposed to the Accountant View, an additional chart will be displayed on the Dashboard. The provided diagram represents the Cash Flow chart. The user has the option to view the financial inflows and outflows over a specified time frame, or they can opt to view the current cash balance.

Having familiarized oneself with the functionality of the user interface in the browser, it is equally worthwhile to explore the interface of the mobile application.

4.2 Targeting Beginners and Small Business Owners

Small business owners often have inquiries regarding accounting and finances unless they are operating an accounting practice. Navigating through the multitude of financial terminology, calculations, and accounting procedures can provide a considerable challenge in maintaining clarity and comprehension. Regardless of whether an individual opts to employ a financial manager or not, possessing a comprehensive understanding of accounting and finance is of utmost importance. Possessing this knowledge base will enable individuals to engage in more effective discourse with their financial experts and make more informed choices. Presented below is a comprehensive manual elucidating financial terminology and procedures that hold significance for proprietors of small enterprises.

Business Accounting Terms

Gaining a comprehension of financial terms can facilitate the process of small business accounting, particularly for individuals responsible for bookkeeping or outsourcing such tasks. The ASPE (Accounting requirements for Private Enterprises) encompasses a comprehensive set of requirements. There are two basic approaches utilized for documenting financial transactions, namely, cash basis and accrual basis. Cash accounting is a method of recording transactions that takes place when cash is exchanged between parties. On the other side, accrual accounting is a method that records transactions as they occur, regardless of when cash is exchanged. Small, unincorporated enterprises frequently exhibit a preference for cash transactions. However, doing a comparative analysis enables one to ascertain the most suitable option. The use of First-In, First-Out (FIFO) accounting, which entails recording sales based on the costs of inventories, also offers advantages.

Debts and Assets

Assets within a corporate entity encompass both intangible assets and contra assets. A comprehensive grasp of debt ratios and asset turnover is of utmost importance. Debt ratios serve as a means to assess the relationship between debts and total assets, while the TIE (times interest earned) metric indicates an entity's capacity to repay its debts. The calculation of the times interest earned (TIE) ratio can be performed using either earnings before interest and taxes (EBIT) or earnings before interest, taxes, depreciation, and amortization (EBITDA). In cases of financial distress, individuals facing overwhelming debt can seek assistance from the licensed insolvency trustee to explore alternatives to filing for bankruptcy.

Financial Reports

The comprehension of financial data holds significant importance for organizations in order to facilitate the process of making well-informed decisions. The standard financial statements commonly utilized in financial reporting encompass balance sheets, income statements, and cash flow statements. Balance sheets provide a comprehensive overview of a company's financial position by presenting its liabilities, assets, and owner's equity. On the other hand, trial balance statements serve the purpose of detecting potential errors in the journal entries made during the accounting process. Bank statements play a crucial role in the effective administration of finances, and conducting weekly reconciliations can serve as a valuable tool for identifying potential problems. The trailing twelve-month (TTM) methodology can be employed to examine the preceding 12-month period. Year-end special reports and cleaning hold significance in the context of preparing for the subsequent year. Online accounting services, such as QuickBooks, can effectively monitor and manage financial data for the purpose of generating accurate financial statements and facilitating routine operational activities.

Revenue and Expenses

Effectively managing business expenses and revenue is essential for achieving success in the corporate realm. The practice of monitoring expenditures is crucial in order to achieve break-even thresholds. The examination of net sales, operating cash flow, and free cash flow facilitates the assessment of profitability. Arrears account balances represent the cumulative amount of outstanding invoices, whereas the aged accounts payable report provides information on forthcoming payments. Net profit margins are indicative of the profitability of a business, whereas free cash flow refers to the amount of cash earned by a company after deducting expenses and reinvesting.

Must-Know Formulas

Quality accounting provides a range of tools that facilitate the establishment of objectives and the evaluation of profitability. These tools encompass a comprehensive comprehension of accounting formulas plus their application.

1. Current Ratio

The current ratio serves as an indicator of the company's financial well-being by assessing the relationship between its current assets and liabilities. The commonly seen value for this metric is often 1.2 or greater, with a ratio under 1 suggesting an inadequate amount of assets for covering liabilities. Lenders commonly want ratios that exceed this threshold.

Current Assets / Current Liabilities = Current Ratio

2. Accounting Equation

The balance sheet equation, also known as the accounting equation, combines the sum of the owner's equity and liabilities to get the total assets of a corporation. Liabilities encompass financial obligations, such as debts, that a company is liable to repay. On the other hand, assets encompass all tangible and intangible resources owned by the organization. Owner's equity refers to the portion of equity that owners and shareholders own.

Liability + Owner's Equity = Assets

3. Variable Cost Ratio

The variable cost ratio is employed by retailers and other entities engaged in the selling of goods to assess the relationship between total variable expenses and net sales.

Variable Costs / Net Sales = Variable Cost Ratio

4. Break-Even Point

The break-even point refers to the stage in which the total sales revenue is equal to the total costs incurred, resulting in neither profit nor loss. The calculation entails the division of fixed costs by the contribution margin and the per unit contribution price. Nevertheless, this particular formula may exhibit limitations when used for fixed costs that experience frequent fluctuations.

Fixed Costs / Contribution Margin = Break-Even Sales Dollars

Fixed Costs / Per Unit Contribution Price = Break-Even Units

5. Contribution Margin

Based on the statement above, it is possible to determine the contribution margin by subtracting the variable cost ratio from 1. According to the formula above, the value is equivalent to 40%. The contribution margin refers to the proportion of each sale that is allocated to the financial performance of a business. But, it refers to the proportion of revenue from a sale that remains after deducting fixed expenditures and can potentially contribute to profits. The following equation represents the formula.

Variable Costs / Net Sales = Contribution Margin

6. Target Net Income

To determine net income, one can utilize the following equation:

Revenues − Expenses = Net Income

In certain instances, it may be desirable to establish a specific aim for net income. It serves as a benchmark for the desired level of income. One may employ the fundamental equation provided and endeavor to identify strategies for augmenting revenue or reducing expenses in order to attain the desired goal of income. However, it may be advisable to disaggregate your objective into sales figures per unit.

7. Gross Margin

In essence, the concept of gross margin involves expressing one's gross earnings as a percentage, providing insight into the proportion of sales that constitutes gross profit. The gross margin can be determined using the following formula:

(Revenue − COGS) / Revenue = Gross Profit Margin

8. Gross Profit

It is important to note that the concept of cost of goods sold (COGS) primarily encompasses the explicit expenses associated with the manufacture of goods. These expenses include but are not limited to labor costs, material costs, equipment costs utilized in the production process, and utility expenses related to the manufacturing facility. The analysis fails to consider additional tax implications or fixed costs.

Gross Profit = Revenue − Cost of Goods Sold (COGS)

9. Price Variance

As previously said, numerous formulas are contingent upon the cost of goods sold (COGS), variable expenses, and direct costs. This formula facilitates the evaluation of the disparity between the factual expenses that have been incurred and the expenses that are being utilized for the computation of gross margins or profits.

(Actual Cost Incurred – Standard Cost) x Actual Quantity = Price Variance

10. Variable Overhead Variance

By utilizing this calculation, one is able to determine the disparity between the actual and predicted variable overhead. Variable costs refer to the expenses that exhibit changes in direct proportion to the level of production output. These costs encompass many elements, such as production supplies, equipment utilities, and labor. In general, it is observed that the costs per unit of commodities tend to decrease as production volume increases, whereas conversely, they tend to increase when production volume decreases. To provide a rudimentary illustration of the occurrence and rationale behind it, consider a scenario in which an individual expends a sum of $100,000 on the lease of specific equipment for one year. When the production quantity reaches 100,000 items, the leasing cost per unit is $1. However, if the production quantity is reduced to only 100 units, the lease cost per unit increases to $1,000. This explanation provides a rudimentary understanding of the rationale for the terminology "variable" for these extra charges.

In order to determine variable overhead efficiency, it is necessary to analyze and allocate both actual and standard overhead costs on a per-labor-hour basis. Subsequently, one may employ the following equation:

Actual Hours Worked x (Actual Overhead Rate – Standard Overhead Rate) = Variable Overhead Spending Variance

11. Efficiency Variance

The efficiency variance provides insight into the disparities between the realized and anticipated utilization of resources, such as supplies or labor. The formula is commonly employed to evaluate the effectiveness of the materials and labor utilized in the manufacturing process. However, it is also applicable in determining the efficiency of services by employing efficiency variance calculations.

The formula for efficiency variance may exhibit slight variations based on the specific aspect being evaluated; nonetheless, the fundamental formula can be expressed as follows:

(Actual Usage or Hours − Standard Usage or Hours) x Standard Rate or Cost = Efficiency Variance

12. Ending Inventory

The term "ending inventory" pertains to the monetary worth of the merchandise that remains in possession after the conclusion of a designated accounting period. The numerical value in question encompasses the entirety of the raw materials, raw materials at various stages of production, and the final products. The assessment of ending inventory can be accomplished by either summing the worth of all objects or by employing the following equation:

COGS − Beginning Inventory − Purchases = Ending Inventory

Business Financing

The growth and expansion of small firms frequently necessitate dependence on external finance sources. Gaining a comprehensive understanding of financial terminology helps facilitate the process of selecting the most suitable financing choice based on individual circumstances. Some potential alternatives for financing include venture capital, which involves providing funds to start-up companies in exchange for equity; adventure capital, which refers to investments made in high-risk ventures with the potential for significant returns; capital markets, which encompass various financial institutions and instruments for raising long-term capital; general security agreements, which are legal contracts that secure a lender's interest in a borrower's assets; short-term financing, which involves obtaining funds for a brief period to meet immediate financial needs; invoice factoring, which entails selling accounts receivable to a third party at a discount; asset-based financing, which involves using assets as collateral to secure a loan; and capital leases, which are long-term leases that give the lessee the opportunity to purchase the leased asset at the end of the lease term. In order to attract potential investors, it is crucial to possess knowledge of the pre-money valuation, which denotes the worth of a firm prior to the infusion of capital. This information facilitates investors in making well-informed judgments and guarantees the acquisition of the requisite working cash for your firm.

Financial Forecasting and Planning

In order to effectively strategize for the future, organizations must strike a harmonious equilibrium between a positive outlook and a realistic assessment while also incorporating robust financial projections. It facilitates the process of making well-informed decisions, forecasting

prospective challenges in cash flow, and comprehending the distinction between linear and exponential growth. The utilization of industry beta, break-even analysis, and Dupont Analysis can effectively contribute to risk management and enhance the overall value of a company. The utilization of historical performance can inform future decision-making processes, specifically in relation to metrics like profitability ratios, gross margin, and income statement estimates. The utilization of payback periods and the compound annual growth rate facilitates the projection of future investment growth. The application of the rule of 72 extends to estimating the timeframe within which investments are expected to double.

Budgeting

The implementation of a master budget is essential for every firm as it serves the purpose of maintaining a favorable cash flow and safeguarding profitability. This tool assists in determining the requisite minimum monthly profit, taking into account one's financial circumstances. The consideration of one's budget is a factor that must be taken into account while determining one's appropriate compensation. One aspect of this issue pertains to the comparative advantages of remunerating oneself through dividends or salary, a determination that may be contingent upon one's financial circumstances. Occasionally, even the most well-crafted budgets deviate from their intended course. Acquiring the knowledge of variance analysis facilitates the examination and evaluation of the disparities between the projected and realized performance in terms of budgetary outcomes.

Pricing and Inventory

Accurate forecasting plays a critical role in the management of physical product sales, as it helps prevent situations of backorders and stock shortages.

Pricing strategies for services and goods encompass the allocation of overhead costs, utilization of the raw materials price index, and computation of the contribution margin.

The categorization of cost behavior aids in the identification and differentiation of variable, fixed, and mixed costs.

The weighted average method takes into consideration the variations in production costs. The practice of job costing involves determining the pricing of services by considering their profitability and also entails comparing the use of variable pricing with absorption costing.

Money Management

The management of working capital plays a vital role in ensuring operational efficiency and achieving business success. In addition, it is crucial to take into account factors such as currency exchange and liquidity. Liquidity ratios aid in assessing a company's ability to cover its debt obligations. Quick ratios are utilized to assess the short-term liquidity of a company, hence revealing the presence of surplus cash or the requirement for additional liquid assets.

Retirement

As an employer, it is advisable to explore retirement savings alternatives such as Registered Retirement Savings Plans (RRSPs) and Group Registered Retirement Savings Plans (GRRSPs) for both yourself and your employees. Investment in an RRSP results in a reduction of income tax liabilities and facilitates the opportunity for employer contributions to be matched. The acquisition of accounting strategies facilitates the process of making informed financial decisions and enhances comprehension of a company's financial state.

Invoicing Clients

Efficiently invoicing clients is of paramount importance for fostering business success. Enhancing comprehension of payment terms and embracing a diverse range of payment alternatives augments the likelihood of expeditious payment. A comprehensive comprehension of Payment Card Industry (PCI) compliance is vital in relation to debit or credit card transactions. The utilization of ratios and computations in the management of accounts receivables facilitates their successful maintenance. The identification of uncollectible debts and the management of reimbursement processes serve to mitigate the financial losses incurred. Moreover, possessing the knowledge of effectively managing refund processes is vital for accurate transaction documentation.

Accounting Help and Audits

Small business self-audits involve the evaluation of accounting and operational procedures to ascertain their level of efficiency and effectiveness. Engaging the services of an accounting company to conduct audits on financial records can be advantageous in the identification of potential issues and the provision of tailored recommendations. Forensic accounting experts can discern both internal and external risks, including cyber theft and theft, in order to conduct a more comprehensive investigation into a given issue.

Small Business Taxes

The implementation of efficient accounting practices throughout the fiscal year serves to streamline the process of tax preparation by effectively recognizing potential deductions and credits. Capital cost allowances are utilized to depreciate significant expenditures, whereas input

tax credits are employed to recover Goods and Services Tax (GST) or Harmonized Sales Tax (HST) payments made on commercial services or goods. The comprehension of business-related choices, such as the utilization of a corporate vehicle vs. a personal vehicle, might have implications on tax liabilities. Small enterprises also encounter the imposition of tariffs and sales tax, necessitating the ability to compute and forecast these expenses in order to enhance financial management. Maintaining precise documentation and comprehending the concept of capital losses and gains can facilitate proactive tax planning.

Hiring a small business accountant

Engaging the services of a small business accountant may improve one's proficiency in bookkeeping, mitigate potential issues, and facilitate more informed financial decision-making. Opting for the services of an accountant with expertise in small business operations might alleviate anxiety. To optimize the duration of interactions with the accountant, it is advisable to employ effective communication techniques and organizational tools such as QuickBooks to streamline document management.

Chapter 5: Recording Income for Retail Businesses

One key distinguishing factor between the retail business model and other models lies in the timing of payment acquisition. Typically, this occurs during the point of sale, which is the moment when products or services must be rendered. The utilization of 30-day payment periods, for instance, is not employed.

This chapter aims to provide instruction on optimizing the settings and capabilities of QuickBooks Online in order to streamline data entry processes and enhance time efficiency.

When configuring QuickBooks Online for a retail enterprise, certain factors should be taken into account, which is particularly relevant to a business strategy centered around retail operations:

- Inventory (stock) requisites

- The process of documenting sales transactions

- The existing mechanisms that may currently be in existence

- The sales environment encompasses physical retail stores, internet platforms, and marketplaces.

- Accepted forms of payment

It is crucial to comprehend the various approaches employed in documenting revenue. The decisions taken will affect the duration needed for both the setup of QuickBooks and the creation of bookkeeping entries. The manner in which sales data is ultimately reported should also be taken into account when determining the method of income recording.

The availability of third-party applications in this domain is on the rise. Upon accessing the QuickBooks applications store (www.apps.com) and conducting a search pertaining to the domains of Retail or E-Commerce, a limited selection of options will be presented for the user's consideration.

The recent acquisition of OneSaas by Intuit suggests that an expansion of capabilities within the Banking part of QuickBooks can be anticipated in the future.

In this chapter, the utilization of applications will be excluded, with an exclusive focus on the tools available within QuickBooks. Applications are highly beneficial and have the potential to significantly enhance efficiency by saving a substantial amount of time. Nevertheless, it is advisable to get a comprehensive understanding of the necessary bookkeeping entries prior to proceeding. It implies that when the magnitude of transactions escalates, it becomes evident which aspects of bookkeeping necessitate time-saving measures.

To commence our analysis, let us direct our attention towards the initial item on our agenda, namely inventory.

5.1 Using Inventory

The utilization of inventory may necessitate thoughtful deliberation in certain instances. The primary objective of utilizing inventory management is to enhance reporting functionalities and ascertain the availability of resale items within the stock.

A small-scale independent merchant operating as a sole proprietorship specializing in the sale of hotdogs may engage in the procurement of hotdogs, condiments, and beverages. There may be limited advantages associated with categorizing these purchases inside the inventory designated for Products and services. Alternatively, purchases can be coded straight to a designated Cost of Sales chart of account category.

Taking into consideration the case of a small-scale sole proprietorship operating a hotdog stand, it is probable that there will be a rapid conversion of inventory from the point of procurement to the point of sale. A larger retail chain operating within a shopping mall is expected to necessitate the implementation of an inventory system due to the procurement of increasing quantities of merchandise.

The potential acquisition of individual things with the intention of reselling them should be taken into consideration. Generating a substantial number of inventory items inside the Products & Services inventory, which are procured and sold just once, may lead to an excessively lengthy inventory roster.

The primary advantage of establishing an inventory item is the potential for enhanced reporting capabilities. The effectiveness of this approach is contingent upon the accurate recording of the sale. In the event that a Product/Service entity is developed specifically for hotdogs, it is imperative to ensure that sales pertaining to this particular item are consistently documented with the corresponding item data. If this action is not taken, it will lead to inflated stock values on the Balance Sheet and exaggerated earnings on the Profit and Loss report.

In order to perform basic accounting tasks, it suffices to utilize the Category information section exclusively. In order to provide comprehensive stock monitoring, it is necessary to encode the purchase information within the designated section for Item details. The inventory functionality, if implemented,

When a feature is being utilized, the items involved may necessitate changes and revaluations of their prices. The section on Considerations for inventory elucidates the mechanisms by which inventory can undergo revaluation, and sales prices can be efficiently updated in large quantities.

After assessing the necessity of inventory tracking, it is vital to deliberate on the methods for recording sales and accepting payments.

5.2 Undeposited funds

In the QuickBooks Online software, users have the option to designate an account with the type of Undeposited money. The account in question possesses a distinct nature to the extent that individuals are restricted to possessing only one.

Payments received can be recorded in Undeposited funds as an alternative to utilizing a bank, thereby serving as a provisional repository for such monies. When the appropriate moment arrives, it is necessary to make a bank deposit in order to transfer funds from the Undeposited funds account.

The designated vocabulary for this particular category of account is commonly referred to as "Undeposited monies." However, it is worth noting that users have the flexibility to modify the name of this account, as exemplified in this instance where it is denoted as "Receipts not yet banked."

Prior to examining the utilization of the Undeposited Money Account, it is necessary to consider a hypothetical scenario wherein a business generates revenue through its website. Payments are directed through several payment systems as a result of the website's construction. These mechanisms include the following:

- PayPal
- Stripe
- American Express
- Direct bank transfers

The funds will be deposited into our business bank account by direct bank transfers. In QuickBooks Online, it is possible to establish supplementary control accounts as banking entities for the purpose of receiving payments using American Express, PayPal, or Stripe.

NUMBER	NAME	TYPE ▲	DETAIL TYPE
1200	1200 Business Bank Account	🏦 Cash at bank and in hand	🏦 Current
1201	1201 American Express	Cash at bank and in hand	Cash on hand
1202	1202 PayPal	Cash at bank and in hand	Cash on hand
1203	1203 Stripe	Cash at bank and in hand	Cash on hand

In order to integrate the utilization of Undeposited cash with the bank accounts established in the preceding screenshot, a Sales receipt should be employed for the purpose of documenting sales.

Consequently, it will be necessary to have a Product/Service item associated with each bank account. Using PayPal as a case study, it is recommended to establish a service item that directs income account transactions to the PayPal bank account.

The tax rate is established as exempt from Value Added Tax (VAT). The significance of this matter lies in the fact that the item in question is solely utilized for the purpose of generating an internal accounting adjustment. The proposed change is not anticipated to have any impact on sales or value-added tax (VAT) revenue.

While not universally required, it is possible to establish an additional category for a chart of accounts and service items in order to effectively track anticipated payments inside a bank account.

The advantage of introducing this supplementary component for direct payments is in its ability to enhance the management of the overall sum, particularly when it comprises different values.

In this particular instance, the complete utilization of Undeposited money is not being achieved due to the fact that the Sales receipt has been reconciled to a balance of £0.00. Consequently, there will be no remaining amount available for deposit.

Similar to our prior analysis, while reviewing the Transaction journal located in the More section, one may observe all the accounting double entries.

ACCOUNT	DEBIT	CREDIT
Receipts not yet banked	£0.00	
Sales		£10,000.00
1202 PayPal	£1,000.00	
1203 Stripe	£700.00	
1201 American Express	£500.00	
1204 Direct payments	£9,800.00	
VAT Control		£2,000.00
	£12,000.00	**£12,000.00**
	£12,000.00	**£12,000.00**

The sale receipt has accurately recorded sales for the purpose of determining profit and loss, and the value-added tax (VAT) due has been appropriately adjusted. Debit entries have been recorded to indicate the sources from which certain payments would be received.

Upon reviewing the bank account, it has been observed that a sum of £8,760 has been received thus far, which falls short of the expected amount of £9,800. Upon careful examination of the bank feed for the Business Account, it is recommended to record this transaction as a transfer originating from the 1204 Direct payments account.

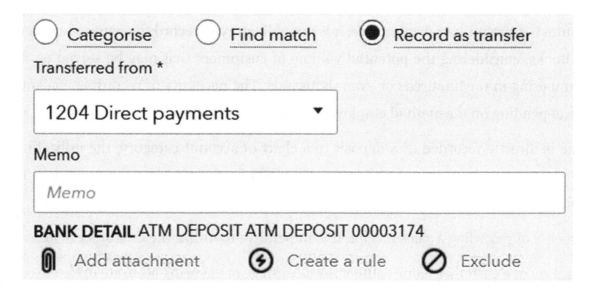

Upon documenting the transaction pertaining to the deposit of monies into the company bank account, it is possible to review the specific information contained within the account about Direct payments.

The shown entries correspond to the £9,800 amount modified on the sales receipt, as well as the £8,760 monies that have been received in the bank account. The remaining amount of £1,040 is expected to be received on the subsequent day.

Now, let us examine an instance in which the Undeposited money account is fully used.

In the present illustration, there exists a miniature café that diligently documents its daily sales. The organization is utilizing a cloud-based point of sale (POS) terminal system. Although there is no integration with QuickBooks, it is still possible to access and download daily sales information. The Electronic Point of Sale (EPOS) system provides the following information.

- Date of sales

- Sales tax information

- The sales details (drinks/foods/takeaway)

- Gratuity

- Methods of payment

5.3 Using Customers

In the context of a retail-based enterprise, it is not obligatory to record the name of each customer in QuickBooks, considering the potential volume of customers that may be served on a weekly basis, numbering in the hundreds or even thousands. The necessity of recording a client's name may vary depending on the method employed for income recording.

If income is directly recorded as a deposit to a chart of account category, the utilization of the Supplier/Customer column is not obligatory. The field in question has the potential to remain unoccupied.

In the process of recording a sales receipt, it is imperative to utilize the Customer field.

The utilization of a customer name confers the advantage of ensuring accurate updates to Sales by Customer reports.

5.4 Sales Environment and other methods of Payment accepted

The confluence of these two factors has led to the integration of these issues, as the prevailing market conditions in which a corporation operates significantly influence the range of payment alternatives employed.

An illustrative instance is the unlikelihood of an online retailer getting payments in the form of cash. Similarly, a business operating a hotdog stand might not experience a substantial influx of payments using PayPal. Nevertheless, the proliferation of mobile payment alternatives like Apple Pay and the growing prevalence of QR codes have significantly enhanced the feasibility of this prospect compared to the situation a few years ago.

Once the method of payment for the sales made by a firm has been determined, the subsequent step is determining the appropriate manner in which the income must be documented within the QuickBooks accounting software. In the retail industry, payment is typically collected at the moment of sale, obviating the need for invoicing.

For the present moment, it is advisable to disregard journal entries and instead consider two alternative methods for documenting income in situations where invoices are not generated. The available options for recording sales proceeds and bank deposits need to be determined.

Bank deposits versus Sales receipts

The choice between utilizing a sales receipt or a bank deposit is contingent upon the reporting obligations imposed on a business. Both alternatives can update the Profit and Loss reports as well as sales taxes, and both have the potential to impact the Sales by Customer reports within the QuickBooks software.

The sole distinction is in the utilization of Product and Service elements inside the sales receipt. The utilization of the Sales receipt option is recommended for individuals seeking to monitor stock amounts, generate gross margin reports, and report on the various categories of goods or services sold.

Additionally, it is noteworthy to mention that the utilization of items and services accompanied by sales receipts allows for a streamlined categorization process, requiring a reduced number of account categories. This phenomenon occurs due to the ability of several items to be allocated to a common profit and loss account for sales, such as the Sales of Product Income account.

Bank Deposits

Income received can be recorded in a selected category of the chart of accounts when utilizing the bank feeds feature in QuickBooks Online.

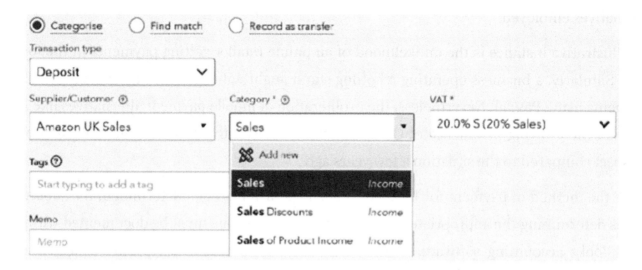

The selection of the customer's name, chart of account type, and VAT rate is possible. The specific amount or visibility of the value-added tax (VAT), which is a form of sales tax, is not discernible on the current display. The reported value always includes the tax component. In the event that the total amount received is £1,800, it will be systematically documented as comprising £1,500 plus an additional £300 in value-added tax (VAT).

In addition to utilizing bank feeds for the purpose of recording bank deposits, QuickBooks Online offers an alternative method through the utilization of the New button. Within this interface, users may access the Bank deposit feature, which is conveniently located below the list of Other alternatives.

The identical entry, whether inputted manually or observed subsequent to being imported from bank feeds.

The value of the Value Added Tax (VAT) can be observed on the Bank Deposit entry screen and can be modified if required.

When opting for a bank deposit, the sum received may not accurately represent the entirety of sales. The quantity in question may be derived from the subtraction of commission or bank charges from the total sales.

In the given scenario, we shall examine the manner in which a sales total of £1,900, inclusive of VAT, can be appropriately adjusted to account for commission charges amounting to £100, which are exempt from VAT.

Splitting bank deposits

In order to incorporate sales and commission charges inside a single bookkeeping entry, it becomes necessary to divide the transaction into numerous lines.

When categorizing transactions from the bank feed, users are provided with the option to split the transaction.

Upon choosing the Split option, users are now able to capture all the necessary facts. The initial line encompasses the aggregate sales amount, inclusive of Value Added Tax (VAT), whereas the subsequent line represents the entire deductions made as negative charges.

Using Sales Receipts

Currently, it is observed that while it is feasible to input a sales receipt directly via the bank feed, the ability to choose the specific product or service is not available. A standardized product/service code must be employed as a default option.

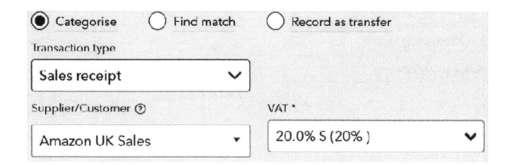

The data entry screen for Sales Receipts closely resembles that of an Invoice. One notable distinction is in the requirement of selecting a Deposit to account when generating a sales receipt, which serves to specify the precise location where cash or card payments are being documented. Invoices are reimbursed in accordance with predetermined conditions, necessitating the inclusion of an anticipated due date.

The current record indicates that a total of three desks and five seats have been successfully sold, resulting in sales amounting to £1,900, inclusive of value-added tax (VAT). There exist charges from Amazon amounting to £100. In order to accurately document financial transactions, it is necessary to record all pertinent values in sales receipts. Thus, it is imperative to include a Service item specifically designated for Amazon charges.

It is recommended that Amazon charges be categorized and recorded as a Cost of Sales in the chart of accounts. The reason for this is that the charge is inherently linked to the act of selling.

When generating a Service item for Amazon charges, the Income account utilized is the Cost of Sales account that has been established.

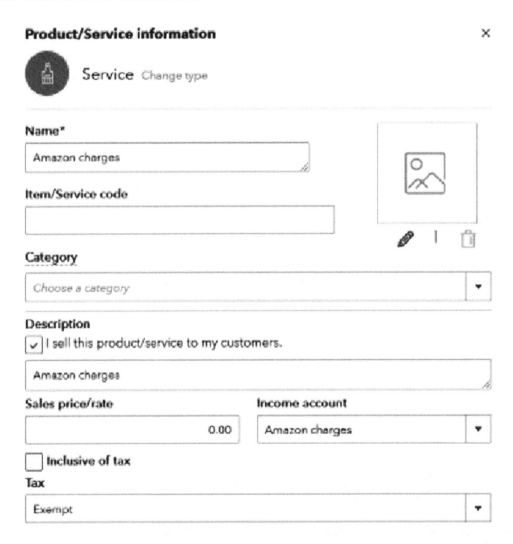

By accessing the Sales receipt interface and navigating to the More option located at the bottom of the data entering the page, users can select the Transaction journal option. This functionality allows for the comprehensive visualization of all recorded entries stemming from the sales receipt.

ACCOUNT	DEBIT	CREDIT
Current	£1,800.00	
Cost of sales	£450.00	
Stock Asset		£450.00
Sales of Product Income		£750.00
Stock Asset		£375.00
Sales of Product Income		£833.33
Cost of sales	£375.00	
Amazon charges	£100.00	
VAT Control		£316.67
VAT Control	£0.00	
	£2,725.00	£2,725.00
	£2,725.00	£2,725.00

In this context, it is evident that by employing various products or services, it becomes feasible to allocate all sales transactions to a single chart of account category, namely Sales of Product Income. The debiting of Amazon commission charges to the Amazon charges category in the Profit and Loss report, as well as the logging of the entire payment amount to the Current bank account, will occur.

5.5 Using journal entries to record sales

In the realm of accounting, it is customary for journal entries to be exclusively employed for the purpose of effecting accounting adjustments so as to rectify discrepancies that manifest in the profit and loss report as well as the balance sheet. In order to comply with the requirements of a journal, it is necessary to include a minimum of one debit entry and one credit entry.

Understanding the use of journal entries holds significance due to the fact that certain third-party applications generate journal entries to mirror the sales data documented in an Electronic Point of Sale (EPOS) system.

To create a journal entry in QuickBooks, users can select the "New" button located on the left navigation menu.

One notable benefit associated with the utilization of a journal entry lies in its capacity to provide prompt visibility into the accounts being employed. In order to ensure accurate accounting of sales tax, it is necessary to utilize the right code when recording sales transactions. The sales tax amount will be displayed as a distinct value in the journal's footer.

However, it is not permissible to utilize Product/Service items while recording a transaction in a journal entry.

For individuals who lack familiarity with journal utilization, it can prove advantageous to develop a template that can be readily employed as necessary.

Recurring entries

The Recurring option is typically located at the lower section of the manual data entry screens. This functionality can be applied to various financial documents such as invoices, sales receipts, bills, expenses, journals, and other similar records.

If the "Scheduled" option is used for the "Type" parameter, the recurring functionality can be utilized to automatically generate an entry at a predetermined interval. If a recurrent entry is stored as "Unscheduled," a template will be retained for future usage as needed.

The Recurring transactions feature may be accessible in QuickBooks by clicking on the gear icon located on the main menu screen, specifically under the LISTS section. After being chosen, all saved templates would be presented. The utilization of a template is possible at any given moment to generate an entry.

Chapter 6: Finding Answers Quickly

In the context of the evolving corporate landscape in the digital age, the utilization of accounting software has emerged as an indispensable instrument for effectively managing financial matters. The introduction of cloud accounting software has enabled businesses to conveniently and flexibly access financial information from any location and at any time, hence offering unprecedented levels of flexibility and convenience. QuickBooks Online represents a cloud-based accounting software solution that has significantly transformed the manner in which enterprises manage their financial operations and find answers quickly.

6.1 The Importance of an Efficient Index

QuickBooks Online offers robust accounting solutions for small and medium-sized enterprises (SMEs). This software facilitates enhanced financial transaction management for enterprises with a comprehensive suite of capabilities, tax compliance, encompassing receipt and invoice monitoring, spending management, and many forms of financial reporting. QuickBooks Online has emerged as a crucial instrument for businesses to effectively administer their financial operations, owing to its intuitive design and robust functionalities.

Through the utilization of cloud computing, enterprises may effectively retrieve their financial data instantaneously, engage in collaborative efforts with their accountants and teams, efficiently oversee their business operations remotely, and significantly enhance overall efficiency and productivity. This section aims to examine the advantages of having unrestricted access to accounting data at any time and from any location. It will also emphasize the role of Intuit QuickBooks Online in assisting businesses in effectively managing their financial matters, facilitating informed decision-making, and enhancing overall efficiency and productivity.

Use QuickBooks accounting software from any location.

One of the primary advantages offered by Intuit QuickBooks Online includes the capability to conveniently retrieve accounting data from any location and at any given moment. The feasibility of this is facilitated by cloud computing, a technology that enables the storage and retrieval of data via the Internet, circumventing the limitations of local computer systems.

When it comes to the management of business finances, utilizing cloud technology offers users a range of significant advantages:

- **Collaboration**

Cloud computing facilitates concurrent access and editing of shared files, hence enhancing collaboration and teamwork among several users. This practice effectively mitigates errors and confusion arising from multiple individuals collaborating in a single location with inadequate communication.

- **Scalability**

In contrast to other accounting systems and services, cloud computing offers businesses the ability to rapidly adjust the scale of their operations in accordance with their requirements without the need for substantial investments in costly hardware or the inefficiencies associated with human data entry.

- **Accessibility**

Cloud computing enables managers to conveniently access data from any location having an internet connection, including the office, home, or while traveling. The significance of this phenomenon in contemporary society lies in the fact that a considerable number of employed people are no longer confined to a fixed workstation during traditional working hours. The popularity of remote and hybrid working models has witnessed a significant surge in the wake of the COVID-19 outbreak. The importance of accessibility lies in its ability to maintain productivity levels while also preserving the flexibility and freedom to move about.

- **Security**

Utilizing cloud computing inherently entails the provision of a comprehensive suite of security measures aimed at safeguarding one's data. These procedures may encompass various security mechanisms, such as encryption protocols, firewalls, and data backups. The importance of safeguarding sensitive information, such as financial data, should not be disregarded or undervalued since it can have significant repercussions on cash flow.

Collaborating with Your Accountant and Team

Collaboration constitutes a fundamental component in the effective operation of a prosperous enterprise. Intuit QuickBooks Online offers collaboration capabilities that facilitate smooth teamwork and communication among organizations, both internally between teams and departments and externally with external parties such as accountants and bookkeepers. These features enable real-time collaboration and information sharing. It implies that universal access to information facilitates the optimization of procedures and mitigates the likelihood of errors. QuickBooks Online facilitates the provision of immediate access to the entirety or a subset of a business's financial data by managers to their accountants. This feature proves advantageous during tax filing processes or while making intricate financial determinations.

Several elements facilitate seamless collaboration with external accountants and team members:

- **Employee access to particular features**

Determine the exact features and places to which employees may be granted access. The system ensures that all individuals are kept informed through user access based on their respective employee levels, allowing them to receive reports and other relevant information without the need to share any login credentials.

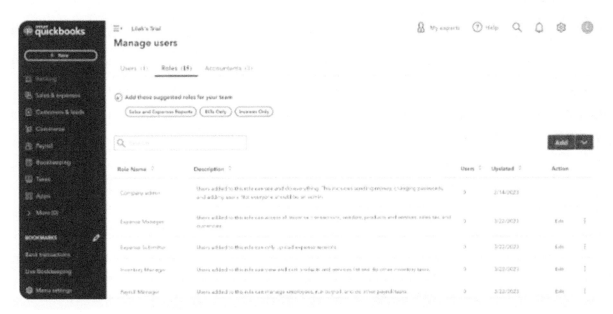

- **Access granted to accountants to books**

Financial reports can be generated and disseminated to accountants, enabling them to provide recommendations that can enhance overall business decision-making. Collaboration between team members and accountants can facilitate the development of a strategic plan aimed at attaining organizational objectives while also enabling the formulation of well-informed judgments grounded in empirical evidence.

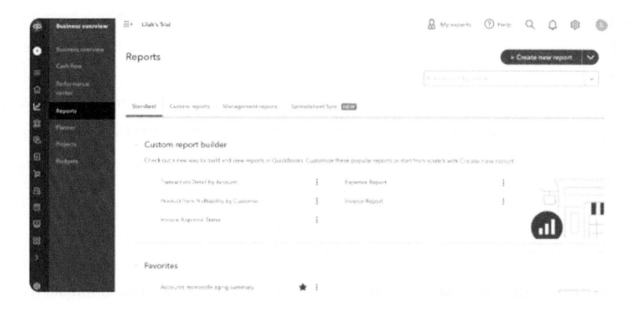

- **Auto-sync**

Financial reporting in QuickBooks Online ensures automatic synchronization across all devices linked to each account. In this manner, all members of the team, as well as other individuals granted access, can be assured that they have access to current information instantaneously. It significantly diminishes the likelihood of duplicating efforts or revising information that has previously been modified.

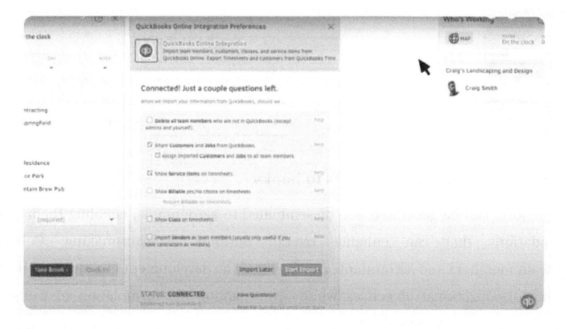

QuickBooks Mobile App

The QuickBooks mobile application enables business owners to effectively oversee all aspects of their business operations using their mobile devices, regardless of their location. Users can input transactions, document expenditures, generate invoices for their clientele, and transmit financial data through the easily navigable mobile application. Similar to the online service, the QuickBooks Mobile App possesses the capability to automatically store all data in the cloud and synchronize it across several selected devices.

Users of QuickBooks Online can utilize a range of beneficial features through the QuickBooks Mobile App. The application provides business owners with the ability to:

- **Invoices are promptly dispatched to the respective customers**

Invoices can be generated through the QuickBooks Mobile App, facilitating their prompt dissemination to customers via email. Android users can transmit invoices using WhatsApp and receive notifications upon their receipt.

- **Monitoring Expenditures Using a Portable Device**

The QuickBooks Mobile App can establish connections with many financial institutions, including bank accounts, credit cards, and other finance applications. Through this integration, the app is able to effectively monitor and record all expenditures and incoming funds, facilitating subsequent bookkeeping processes.

- **Accepting card payments**

The application incorporates a portable card reader capable of instantly accepting payments made through credit cards. Subsequently, the payment is duly documented, and the funds are automatically delivered to the bank account linked to the application.

- **Attaching receipts to invoices**

The process of scanning and inputting receipts can be facilitated through the utilization of the camera feature available on many mobile devices. The application will promptly authorize all transactions and, after that, document the billable expense. Reimbursements and tax deductions can be effectively monitored by associating receipts with invoices.

- **Provide estimations**

The QuickBooks Mobile App can generate professional estimates, which may include blueprints, photo attachments, or contracts. The application allows for the direct transmission of a duplicate document to customers via email, while customers who are physically there can promptly acknowledge and affix their signature.

Backup and Security

When considering sensitive financial information, ensuring security is of utmost importance. QuickBooks Online prioritizes security and implements multiple safeguards to ensure the protection of user data. QuickBooks Online, being a cloud-based service, employs (128-bit SSL) sophisticated encryption technology alongside additional security precautions such as password-protected login and firewall-protected servers. Furthermore, the software utilizes routine security audits conducted by its internal staff and specialized tools to guarantee the continuous protection of all data.

In addition to ensuring data security, QuickBooks Online also implements a comprehensive backup system. The implementation of automatic daily backups alleviates concerns among managers regarding potential data loss resulting from system crashes or other unanticipated complications. QuickBooks Online employs a distributed storage system across numerous secure data centers, ensuring the preservation of financial data integrity and accessibility from any location while maintaining a high level of security.

QuickBooks Online incorporates the utilization of the Always-On Activity Log, which serves as a comprehensive log documenting all user activities, and the Audit Trail, which maintains a historical record of all modifications made to individual transactions. It is important to note that both capabilities are permanently enabled and cannot be disabled by any user. The capabilities above are designed to capture and document each instance of user login as well as any modifications performed to the financial transaction. In this manner, no alterations can occur to all records without triggering an alert, and a physical document will exist to track all actions back to their initial source.

Increased Productivity and Efficiency

The ability to access accounting data remotely and at any given time can greatly enhance the efficiency and production of an organization. QuickBooks Online offers businesses the opportunity to optimize their financial procedures, resulting in a significant reduction in manual data input and the automation of repetitive and labor-intensive activities.

As an illustration, rather than engaging in the manual input of data from individual paper receipts or invoices, QuickBooks Online offers users the capability to capture an image of the document through the application. Subsequently, the software autonomously extracts the relevant data and generates a corresponding record.

The automation of laborious operations, such as the entering of data, tracking of invoices, and reporting of receipts, results in significant time savings and a substantial decrease in the likelihood of errors committed by humans going unnoticed. Collaboration is facilitated by the seamless accessibility of crucial financial data in real-time, hence enhancing the ease of coordination among team members. The implementation of this approach enhances the efficiency of communication and reduces the duration required to accomplish activities. The enhancement of financial data accessibility through cloud-based online and mobile platforms enables users to do operations remotely and make prompt judgments, free from the constraints of a fixed workspace.

6.2 A Valuable Resource for Desktop Users

QuickBooks Online plus QuickBooks Desktop exhibit similar features and functionalities, catering to the operational requirements of businesses.

Let us conduct a more detailed examination of some of these distinctions.

1. Accessibility

A notable distinction between QuickBooks Desktop and QuickBooks Online is in their accessibility. QuickBooks Online offers the convenience of accessing the software via internet-enabled device, regardless of time and location. In contrast, QuickBooks Desktop necessitates installation on a specific PC.

QuickBooks Online exhibits compatibility with a diverse array of web browsers, encompassing Google Chrome, Mozilla Firefox, and Microsoft Edge. Additionally, the platform offers a mobile application that is compatible with both Android and iOS operating systems.

Although the usage of QuickBooks Desktop has been limited to the total of installations provided in the chosen service tier, it is possible to utilize the hosting provider that access the desktop software over the cloud server. By utilizing a unique password and username, individuals are able to authenticate their identity and gain remote access to their files and data, mirroring the experience of accessing such resources via the local desktop environment.

It is important to mention that QuickBooks Desktop has been exclusively compatible with Windows operating systems. In order to utilize the service, individuals who utilize Mac operating systems would be required to subsequently install and download QuickBooks for Mac.

2. Integrations

QuickBooks Online features additional third-party integrations rather of its desktop counterpart. That interacts with more than 750 common business applications and platforms, automating and simplifying numerous accounting operations. It also features a lot simpler connecting procedure, enabling you to access third-party programs immediately online.

Inside the app store having extra connections accessible, QuickBooks Online integrations hold a larger series of business requires and offer many payment gateway possibilities.

As a result, a lot of the QuickBooks Desktop connectors are focused on ecommerce. It offers restricted payment channels, rendering it hard for modern firms to collect online invoice payments.

Although it owns less option accessible, QuickBooks Desktop interfaces with more than 200 third-party programs, representing it among the networked desktop software solutions.

3. Tiers and Pricing

QuickBooks Online offers a selection of four distinct monthly plans tailored to meet the needs of businesses, with each plan offering a predetermined allocation of user accounts. In contrast, QuickBooks Desktop is offered as the yearly subscription, accompanied by an incremental charge for each client. QuickBooks Online offers a complimentary trial period of 30 days. However, QuickBooks Desktop has a refund policy allowing customers to receive their money back within 60 days.

The pricing structure of QuickBooks Online may be more suitable for individuals seeking a stable monthly payment plan. This solution is particularly advantageous for enterprises that may operate without incurring the costs associated with a yearly subscription and supplementary charges for each user.

While, in the scenario where there is single user and a need for advanced features and software that's locally installed, QuickBooks Desktop emerges as the more suitable option. It is important to note that the supplementary fees associated with QuickBooks Desktop have the potential to accumulate rapidly, especially in cases where several users are involved.

4. Ease of use and installation

The consideration of ease of use has significant importance while selecting a software product. The installation process for QuickBooks Desktop on a single computer is typically a brief task, requiring only a few minutes. However, when installing the software on numerous computers, the complexity increases due to the necessity of granting each machine access to the corporate data file.

Due to its cloud-based nature and lack of installation requirements, QuickBooks Online emerges as the unequivocal victor in terms of installation convenience.

Furthermore, it may be argued that QuickBooks Online offers a higher level of user-friendliness and navigational ease compared to QuickBooks Desktop, mostly due to its simplified and intuitive user interface. The mobile app and online dashboard exhibit notable ease of comprehension and usability owing to their visually intuitive and unambiguous graphical interface.

On the other hand, QuickBooks Desktop was specifically developed with a focus on catering to the needs of accounting professionals. The software possesses a menu designed in a flowchart-style format, allowing users to navigate through many options. Additionally, the user interface may be customized according to individual preferences, and the software also offers shortcuts for frequently utilized features.

5. Reporting options

Comprehensive reporting tools are included in all versions and plans of QuickBooks. However, it should be noted that QuickBooks Desktop is the only version that provides industry-specific reports tailored for retail, manufacturing, nonprofit, wholesale, and professional services sectors.

QuickBooks Online offers a range of more than 80 reports, contingent upon the individual plan chosen. In contrast, QuickBooks Desktop Enterprise and Premier Plus plans allow access to a broader selection of over 150 industry-specific documents. In addition to its core functionalities, QuickBooks Desktop offers supplementary capabilities that enable users to personalize and export reports according to their requirements.

QuickBooks Desktop being particularly well-suited for:

- **Thorough inventory accounting:** Organizations that engage in intensive inventory accounting offer a comprehensive inventory management and accounting solution.

- **Bookkeeping for various businesses:** In the absence of the requirement for integrated financial statements, QuickBooks Desktop can be utilized to effectively handle the accounting records for an endless number of organizations.

- **Specialized industries:** QuickBooks Desktop is well-suited for specialist businesses, like retailers and nonprofit organizations, who seek customized industry-specific solutions.

QuickBooks Online is particularly well-suited for:

- **Ecommerce businesses:** Due to its easy integration with various ecommerce platforms. As a result, it is widely regarded as the most highly recommended accounting software for web-based or smaller enterprises operating in the ecommerce sector.

- **Cloud-based accounting:** Cloud-based accounting is a convenient solution for businesses and mobile entrepreneurs that prioritize managing their operations through smartphones. QuickBooks Online allows users to view their accounts from any internet-connected computer or mobile device.

- **For businesses that require numerous users,** QuickBooks Online is recommended as it allows for the provision of access to more than one individual, including tax professionals or independent accountants. In the case of QuickBooks Desktop, supplementary charges are incurred for the purpose of granting access to a greater number of users.

BOOK THREE

Chapter 7: Meeting the Needs to Success with Projects

Projects serve as an excellent means of assessing the financial viability of individual tasks undertaken for clients. The utilization of projects in QuickBooks is commonly linked to the building sector by individuals; nonetheless, it is important to note that several types of businesses might derive advantages from employing this functionality.

Various professional service providers, such as marketing firms, lawyers, graphic designers, as well as accountants and bookkeepers, often engage in distinct forms of work for a shared consumer or client. Utilizing project management techniques to maintain distinct records of individual tasks facilitates the streamlined assessment of the financial viability of certain undertakings.

Settings for Projects

This section will examine the essential configurations required to optimize the utilization of Projects in QuickBooks Online. The proposed system will incorporate functionalities for monitoring and categorizing expenditures based on client or project, as well as facilitating the utilization of the Progress Invoicing feature in instances where several invoices are required for a single estimate.

Firstly, it is imperative to verify whether the project functionality has been activated.

Settings to track expenses by customer

There will probably be a need for some supplementary configurations. The subsequent configurations to verify are located within the Expenses section.

By configuring the settings as depicted, it will be possible to allocate project expenses accurately.

In conjunction with assigning a cost to a client, there exist possibilities to designate expenditures and goods as billable, as well as incorporate a default markup rate if deemed necessary. These functions can prove to be beneficial in cases where a customer necessitates more charges for recharging, along with an estimate that might have previously been dispatched.

Prior to concluding our examination of Account and Settings, there remains another setting that warrants attention. This particular setting proves advantageous in cases where invoicing for our projects occurs at various stages of completion.

Enabling Projects

The Projects feature is often activated by default in QuickBooks Online and may be accessed through the Left Navigation panel. Suppose a user has an active Plus subscription and cannot instantly locate the Projects function. In that case, they can enable it by accessing the Advanced section inside the Account and Settings menu.

By selecting the firm name displayed on the Dashboard, users can access the Account and Settings section immediately.

The utilization of Projects serves the objective of monitoring the profitability in relation to a certain task or assignment. Accurate tracking of expenses and products necessitates the adoption of a system that enables the monitoring of customer-specific transactions. Therefore, it is imperative to verify that the parameters above have been properly configured.

Progress Invoicing

The Sales tab within the Account and Settings interface provides users with the ability to utilize the feature known as Progress Invoicing. This functionality enables the user to generate a comprehensive and consolidated estimate, which may be subsequently invoiced at various milestones throughout the completion of the project.

The utilization of this particular feature will be deferred until the subsequent portion of this chapter, namely the segment pertaining to Recording Income and Expenditure against a Project.

Having ensured that all the necessary settings have been enabled for projects, we're ready to proceed and establish a project for one of our clients.

7.1 Creating a Project

Utilizing a project framework for a client facilitates a clear distinction between various tasks that may be undertaken for a singular client. An illustration will be provided using the context of an advertising and marketing agency.

The organization is currently engaged with a client involved in the production and distribution of health food supplements. Specifically, the client has recently developed a novel protein shake and is seeking assistance in its promotional endeavors.

The production of pamphlets and website advertising banners will necessitate design work, which incurs time costs. Additionally, the agency will engage suppliers for printing plus other advertising charges, resulting in bills and expenses.

The agency will generate a cost estimation for the completion of the task. Once the preliminary concept has been formulated, half of the total work will be billed, while the remaining portion will be invoiced upon completion of the task.

Prior to undertaking any of the tasks above, it is important to establish our project, a process that may be effortlessly accomplished. To access the Projects section, please navigate to the Left Navigation panel and select the appropriate option. In the event that this is the initial undertaking, a comprehensive instructional manual will be provided to facilitate the commencement of the project. If any prior projects have been established, users will have the ability to access a visible option for initiating a new project located on the right-hand side of your screen.

When either option is chosen, the essential information needed is a project name with the name of the customer associated with the project. Supplementary notes may be included if deemed relevant.

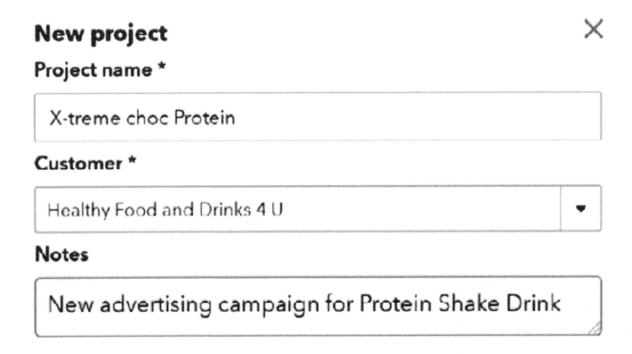

After the act of saving the recently generated project, the user is promptly redirected to the Overview section of the Project. At this juncture, the summary will accurately exhibit a value of £0.00 for INCOME, COSTS, and PROFIT, given the absence of any transactions conducted thus far.

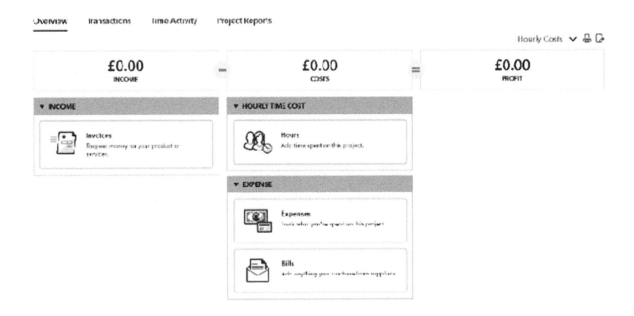

The Overview section contains shortcuts that can be utilized to generate entries for the Project, specifically pertaining to the INCOME and COSTS variables. The utilization of shortcuts facilitates the generation of invoices, documentation of bills and expenses, as well as the recording of hours expended by employees or sub-contractors.

Prior to commencing the recording of any revenue or expenses pertaining to this project, we must transmit a formal estimate to the client delineating the anticipated scope of work. First, let us examine the process of doing that task.

7.2 Recording Time against a Project

There are several advantages to having employees or sub-contractors document their time in QuickBooks. In addition to facilitating the generation of a more accurate profit estimate for a given project, cost analysis can also assist business owners in determining the appropriate pricing strategy for subsequent comparable endeavors. Furthermore, in the absence of a predetermined fixed rate for a project, the duration of time expended can be deemed billable and, therefore, invoiced to the client.

Who can measure and document the passage of time?

Individuals who possess the necessary authorization to utilize QuickBooks can log time dedicated to a certain job. It is feasible to develop a user with restricted access solely to the capabilities related to Time tracking. To include new users in the system, one must navigate to the gear icon and, after that, choose the "Manage users" option.

Users who exclusively engage in time-tracking activities are not included in the user limitations, hence providing a significant advantage.

Prior to examining the methods of time recording, it is necessary to establish a suitable setup for employees and sub-contractors.

Sub-Contractors and Employees

Employees and subcontractors can log their working hours in QuickBooks, provided that they have been authorized to do so. In the absence of utilizing QuickBooks Online payroll software, it is still possible to include employees within the Payroll section of QuickBooks.

The Payroll section can be accessed through the left-hand navigation panel within QuickBooks. In the event that an employee is recruited, there exists the possibility of specifying the cost rate per hour plus the billing rate per hour for that person.

In addition, it is feasible to incorporate hourly cost rates into the Projects Center, which serves as a comprehensive repository for all listed projects. Located in the upper right-hand corner of your screen, users will discover the option to access the Hourly Cost Rate. By selecting that particular option, you will be able to utilize the "+ Add Employee" function to include other employees who may not now be visible.

In the event that an employee is included in your project area but lacks a designated cost rate, the opportunity to incorporate one is accessible. The pencil icon provides the functionality to modify the rates. Once the user has chosen either choice, they will have access to the Hourly Cost Rate Calculator icon, which can assist in formulating a suggested hourly cost rate for an employee.

Sub-contractors can be defined as suppliers or vendors within the QuickBooks software. When making modifications to supplier information, it is feasible to make adjustments to the supplier's hourly billing and cost rates. In the event that expenses are assigned to a certain project, it may not be imperative to utilize the cost rate, being the bill inherently represents the cost incurred by the subcontractor.

The utilization of recording time is particularly advantageous for enterprises in which a significant portion of expenses is attributed to the number of hours dedicated to project completion. In service-oriented industries, such as those involving lawyers, accountants, and consultants, there is typically no expenditure on physical materials. By including costs that are directly associated with the duration of a project, a more precise assessment of the project's profitability can be obtained.

After acquiring knowledge on the establishment of hourly rates for employees and sub-contractors, let us now examine the process of recording time.

Timesheet Entries

In the project overview, a shortcut is provided underneath the COSTS figure for Hours. One may initiate the recording of time by simply selecting this option with a click.

Upon choosing the designated function to incorporate hours from your project overview, users will encounter a display interface that allows for the recording of time pertaining to a singular day. The process involves inputting the employee or supplier/vendor's name, together with the corresponding cost rates and the project name associated with the completed task. Time can be expressed in two ways: as a numerical value representing the number of hours or by specifying the start and finish timings.

 When work is billed on an hourly basis rather than a fixed sum based on an estimate, the duration of time spent on the task can be designated as chargeable. It can be observed that the Billable checkbox has been left unmarked, indicating that the recorded time is not eligible for billing purposes, aligning with the previously agreed upon estimate.

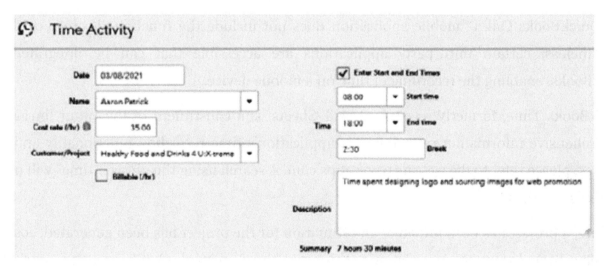

The QuickBooks software offers time tracking options within the EMPLOYEES column, which may be accessed through the New button located in the left-hand navigation panel. The option depicted is equivalent to a one-time activity. The Weekly Timesheet feature facilitates the consolidation of all weekly work hours into a single interface.

Weekly Timesheet

Aaron Patrick ▼	2/8/2021 to 8/8/2021 ▼

#	DETAILS		MON 2	TUE 3	WED 4
1	Healthy Food and Drinks 4 U:X-Treme Choc ▼ Cost rate (/hr) 🛈 35.00 Time spent designing logo and sourcing maqes for web promotion	☐ Billable (/hr)	5.00	7.30	5.00

With the availability of recorded time data, it is now possible to reevaluate the profit values associated with the project. The duration of the recording will not affect the overall financial performance of the firm. However, it will influence the profitability of a specific project, particularly once hourly cost rates are taken into consideration.

The decrease in recorded employee time has resulted in a reduction of £612.50 in profit for this particular task, as it corresponds to the expenses incurred for the hours worked by the employees.

The QuickBooks Online mobile application does not include the functionality to record time. Nevertheless, certain third-party applications are accessible that can be integrated with QuickBooks, enabling the recording of time on a mobile device.

QuickBooks Time, formerly recognized as T-Sheets, is a constituent of the Intuit lineage. For comprehensive information regarding this application's time recording functionality and other features, please refer to the website www.apps.com. A search using the phrase "time" will provide the necessary details.

To date, a project has been initiated, an estimation for the project has been generated, costs and time have been documented in relation to this project, and an invoice has been sent for 50% of the initial estimated value. The implementation of a budget can prove beneficial in maintaining a vigilant oversight of projected expenditures and revenues.

Let us examine the operational mechanisms of QuickBooks.

7.3 Recording Expenditure and Income against a Project

In this illustrative instance, we will generate a quotation that will be dispatched to the client and subsequently designated as approved within the QuickBooks software platform. While the use of estimates is not obligatory, they can be valuable and serve as a valuable starting point. Let us now proceed with the discussion.

Creating an Estimate

To initiate the process, access the action menu labeled "Add to project" while having a project open. At this juncture, the user will be able to locate the option for generating an estimate.

For those who have not previously utilized estimates, the visual layout closely resembles that of the invoice. One distinguishing factor is the inclusion of payment terms and an anticipated due date in invoices, whereas estimates can be stored with the expiration date.

An estimate refers to a non-posting entry in accounting. It implies that the generation of an estimate would not affect the financial documentation of a company until it is transformed into an invoice.

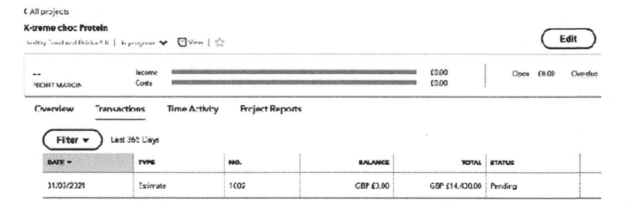

The diagram illustrates the transactions that have been incorporated into the project, which currently consists solely of the estimate. The estimation has had no impact on the project's revenue.

The status of an estimate can be modified at any given moment by selecting the drop-down action menu associated with the estimate. The available status options include Pending, Accepted, Closed, and Rejected. The estimate's status will transition to "Closed" automatically upon full invoicing.

With our estimate agreed, work on a project will commence, and this may involve paying charges on behalf of the customer. Let's see what occurs when we've got a handful of supplier bills that have to be related to a project.

Allocating Expenses and Bills to a Project

The figure illustrates the necessary configurations that must be activated in order to appropriately link expenses with a specific client or project. Once these settings have been implemented, users will have access to supplementary fields when creating bills, expenses, or checks.

In order to assign a cost to a project, it is sufficient to fill out simply the CUSTOMER/PROJECT box. Nevertheless, if there is a cost that must be added to the original estimate, it ought to be designated as billable and may include a markup percentage if deemed necessary.

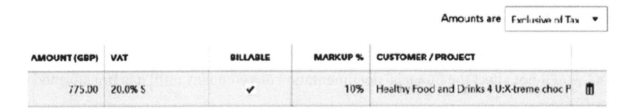

AMOUNT (GBP)	VAT	BILLABLE	MARKUP %	CUSTOMER / PROJECT	
775.00	20.0% S	✔	10%	Healthy Food and Drinks 4 U:X-treme choc P	🗑

In situations when uncertainty arises over the appropriateness of designating a cost as billable, it is advisable to opt for selecting the corresponding checkbox as a precautionary measure. A tool exists that can be utilized to reconcile any remaining unbilled expenses. This topic will be examined in the section titled "Managing Unbilled Expenses."

An additional expense has been incurred for the project we are now engaged in. However, it is worth noting that the fields pertaining to billable hours and markup percentages have been left blank.

Currently, we have formulated a project estimate and accrued expenses that are linked to the project. Let us examine the manner in which the transactions manifest themselves within the project.

Filter ▼   Last 365 Days

DATE ▼	TYPE	NO.	BALANCE	TOTAL	STATUS
03/08/2021	Bill		GBP £930.00	GBP £930.00	Open
03/08/2021	Billable Expense Charge		GBP £0.00	GBP £852.50	Open
01/08/2021	Bill		GBP £3,000.00	GBP £3,000.00	Open
31/07/2021	Estimate	1002	GBP £0.00	GBP £14,400.00	Pending

The view presents the transaction values in their gross form, which includes any applicable VAT or sales tax, with the exception of the billable expense charge. This statement illustrates the suggested reimbursement to the consumer for the expenses accrued in Figure 6.10. The sum of £775, combined with a 10% surcharge of £77.50, results in a cumulative cost of £852.50.

It is now necessary to generate an invoice for the initial 50% of the original estimation. In order to have a comprehensive understanding, let us examine the mechanics of its functionality.

Creating invoices against a Project

In QuickBooks, various pathways exist that finally converge at the same input screen, mirroring the multifaceted nature of the software.

The diagram illustrates an approximate value that is perceptible within the Transactions section of a certain project. The Create Invoice option, located on the far right, will be utilized in this particular illustration.

When Progress Invoicing is enabled, the screen will be displayed in the manner depicted in the accompanying screenshot.

How much do you want to invoice?

○ Remaining total of all lines

◉ | 50% | of each line = | £7,200.00 |

○ Custom amount for each line

Create invoice

Upon choosing the alternative to generate an invoice for 50% of the initial estimate, we proceeded to select the option to create the invoice. The invoice screen will be accessed, providing the opportunity to make any necessary modifications.

In this particular instance, a chargeable expense has been generated, which will be displayed on the right-hand side of the screen, providing us with the opportunity to include it in the invoice.

In the present scenario, it is advisable to refrain from imposing any further charges above the initial estimate. Consequently, the consideration of this billable expense will be disregarded at this time.

Upon incorporating income and expenditure data into QuickBooks for the project, the Overview page will undergo several modifications.

All statistics presented in the overview are displayed as net, excluding any applicable value-added tax (VAT) or sales tax.

Currently, our project is demonstrating a profit of £2,725. To what extent can the accuracy of this figure be ascertained? What would be the implications if there were employees involved in the execution of this project? The maximization of productivity and profitability necessitates the meticulous documentation of employees' project-related labor hours, as time holds an intrinsic value akin to monetary resources.

This analysis will examine the various components associated with the process of documenting staff hours allocated to a certain project.

7.4 Creating a Budget against a Project

In order to formulate the budget, it is necessary to consider factors beyond the confines of the project area. The Budgeting feature may be accessed by selecting the gear icon located at the top right corner of the main screen and, after that, navigating to the TOOLS choices.

In the event that it is the initial budget, a budget creation button will be located at the center of the screen. If a budget has been established in advance, the option to Add a budget will be perceptible in the upper right-hand corner of the budget interface.

The process of developing a budget is generally uncomplicated. Upon the creation of the budget, the options above will be prominently shown at the uppermost section of the screen.

- **Name:** It is necessary to assign a name to the budget.

- **Interval:** The user is required to input budget numbers at regular intervals, specifically on a monthly, quarterly, or yearly basis. Regardless of the chosen interval, the system will generate monthly figures for reporting purposes proportionate to the selected interval.

- **Financial Year:** Please select the fiscal year to which the budget pertains.

- **Pre-filling data:** It is possible to opt for the inclusion of real values, but this is typically not necessary for most projects.

- **Subdivided by:** To establish a budget for a project, it is necessary to choose the customer and subdivide accordingly.

- **Add subdivided budget for:** Please include a detailed breakdown of the budget for the specific project you are preparing the budget for.

Once the appropriate parameters have been chosen for the budget, users will be able to proceed by clicking on the "Next" button located in the bottom right-hand corner of the initial budget screen.

On the subsequent display, users can input anticipated revenue and expenditure figures corresponding to the specified categories. When developing a budget for the project, it is advisable to limit the number of categories being utilized. (Positive values are used for all quantities entered.)

When engaging in the process of budget editing, it is worth noting the presence of a cog icon located on the rightmost side of the screen. This feature allows for the modification of the budget's visualization and the concealment of any unused rows.

After inputting all the anticipated income and expenses into a budget, if one is satisfied with the established values, it is possible to achieve savings in the budget.

The list of created budgets will include all budgets that must be saved. Various activities can be undertaken in relation to stored budgets, with particular emphasis placed on the Run Budgets vs. Actuals report option, which is of primary relevance to us.

By choosing the Run Budget vs. Actuals report option, we may assess our performance in relation to our anticipated outcomes. Merely opting for this particular choice in isolation will not yield the intended report sought, necessitating some degree of modification.

Once the user has chosen the "Run Budgets vs. Actuals" report, they should proceed by selecting the "Customize" option located in the upper right-hand corner of your screen.

In this particular instance, two modifications are being implemented at the outset:

- **Filter:** The filter is used to choose the customer, which is identified by the project name.

- **Column/Rows:** The modification of the "Show Grid" feature to present the comparison between Accounts and Total in terms of rows and columns.

By customizing the report in this manner, we will obtain a Budget against the Actuals report that will enhance visual comprehension. The provided screenshot illustrates the anticipated presentation of the report, incorporating the modifications above. It is important to note that a multitude of alternatives exist in terms of customization.

The report indicates that 50% of our revenue has been invoiced, aligning with our anticipated projections. However, there exist more domains that do not align with our allocated financial resources. The observed discrepancy may be attributed to variations in timing or overlooked expenses.

At present, we will deem the data as satisfactory, and we can subsequently reassess the report to ascertain the absence of any substantial expenditure exceeding the allocated budget.

When generating and personalizing reports, it is important to remember to use the option to save the customization. By utilizing the Custom Reports feature inside the Reports section, you will have the capability to efficiently rerun the report at a later time.

In the preceding section, expenses were accrued and designated as chargeable. The data indicates that there is a project cost of £775, which has been identified for reimbursement to the customer with an additional 10% markup.

In the event that an erroneous billing designation has been applied, it is possible to rectify the situation by making an adjustment to the transaction and deselecting the checkbox labeled "BILLABLE." This scenario would provide a challenge if a substantial number of transactions were erroneously generated across various clients and projects.

There exists a discreet utility that can be employed to efficiently modify numerous transactions simultaneously.

7.5 Managing Unbilled Expenses

When an expense, bill, or check is designated as "BILLABLE," it will consistently be displayed on the right-hand side of the screen throughout invoice creation, thereby asking the user to include the associated cost in the invoice.

The unrecorded expense will also be visible in the Unrecorded Time and Expenses report, which is included in the Project Reports section of a project. The displayed values will be limited to those pertaining to the specific project.

To retrieve a comprehensive overview of unbilled charges on all clients, users can navigate to the left-hand navigation panel and reach the Reports section. From there, they can search specifically for the "Unbilled charges" report. This report will provide detailed information on all outstanding charges that have not yet been billed.

Upon selecting the Unbilled Charges report, it is observed that the default setting of the report is to exhibit unbilled charges for all clients across all dates.

The report displays two clients that have incurred a limited number of Billable Expenses. Even with this limited number of entries, the task of editing and deselecting the billable expense box would be cumbersome. Consider the potential time required to complete such a task with several hundred items.

Using the manage billable expense tool

The option for managing billable expenses cannot be located within any available menus. The exclusive means of accessing it entails modifying the address bar inside the web browser. All content following the term "app" should be eliminated and substituted with "managebillableexpense."

After modifying the browser URL, a distinct interface will appear, prompting the user to provide a certain date that QuickBooks will utilize to conceal any outstanding charges that have not yet been billed.

After the selection of the date, users can proceed by clicking on the Save option located at the lower right corner of the screen. This utility effectively eliminates the "billable" designation from previously generated transactions.

After successfully documenting project transactions and rectifying any erroneously indicated billable charges, it is vital to explore additional reports that prove valuable in project management.

Chapter 8: Going Beyond the Basics – Improving the Integrity of Your Financial Statements

In line with our ongoing examination of our accounting entries, it may be necessary to implement some improvements. Currently, we have completed the fundamental aspects, which entail ensuring the comprehensive reconciliation of bank accounts and verifying the accuracy and currency of customer and supplier balances.

The analysis will commence by examining prevalent errors associated with the chart of accounts, rectifying them, and subsequently assessing the impact of these corrections.

8.1 Common Errors Linked with Chart of Accounts

It is advisable to maintain a simplified chart of accounts and minimize the utilization of account categories whenever feasible. Nevertheless, there will probably come a point in time when there appears to be an absence of a suitable classification for the transaction that one is attempting to document.

When entries are being recorded via the bank feed and the user chooses to add a new category, the default Account Type will be "Cash at bank and in hand."

A user without experience or hastily creating accounts may inadvertently generate a new chart of account categories having an inaccurate type.

The inclusion of the new account example was necessitated by the necessity to document the payment of £3,458.30 for Recruitment Expenses. If an inappropriate Account Type is utilized, the corresponding entry would not affect the Profit and Loss statement and would instead be reflected on our Balance Sheet as a bank account.

It is imperative to thoroughly examine each value in relation to every category pertaining to Profit and Loss and Balance Sheet. This scrutiny is necessary not only to verify the accuracy of the presented data but also to ascertain their appropriate placement within the designated report and section thereof.

The selection of Detail Type in QuickBooks Online has implications for the grouping of figures in tax returns generated using the software, although it is important to note that this option may change across different locations. In the context of utilizing a third-party application for the generation of tax returns and financial statements, the accurate configuration of the Detail Type feature is also beneficial.

In cases when an account must be established erroneously, it is feasible to modify the account to the appropriate classification, albeit with certain limits that may impede the process. In the event that a type is modified, a warning will be issued.

In order to ensure the accurate generation of reports in QuickBooks, it is necessary to accept the warning that facilitates the appropriate placement of Recruitment Expenses within the Profit and Loss statement rather than the Balance Sheet.

After doing a thorough examination of the Profit and Loss statement and Balance Sheet, it is evident that each of the categories currently employed possess the appropriate Account Type. Consequently, our next step involves assessing if we have an excessive number of categories in use.

8.2 Common Errors Linked with Services and Products

Every item in the inventory, as well as all services offered, is associated with a minimum of one category in the chart of accounts. The primary application of a Product or Service item is in the context of generating an invoice, as it is not feasible to directly assign an invoice to a specific chart of account code.

One advantage of utilizing a Product or Service item is the ability to offer a wide range of services while consolidating the corresponding sales statistics under a single chart of account categories, such as the Sale of Products or Fees.

When it comes to QuickBooks reporting, business owners may opt to utilize many charts of account categories in order to accurately represent various sources of income. The execution of such a task is deemed unnecessary given the availability of alternative methods, such as generating reports such as the Sales by Product/Service Summary.

It has been observed that certain items pertaining to Products/Services are being allocated to an incorrect category within the chart of accounts. Upon selecting the value of 50,581 inside Billable Expenses Income, it becomes apparent that expenditures related to food and venue rental are erroneously being credited to this account instead of being appropriately allocated to the Services account.

In order to rectify these entries, it is necessary to make modifications to the Product/Service item. Specifically, the Income account should be revised to "Services," and it is important to verify that the "Also update this account in past transactions" box is selected.

Upon modifying the Product/Service items pertaining to Catering and Venue Rental to utilize the Income account, specifically designated as Services, and opting to simultaneously update this account in past transactions, the Profit and Loss report exhibits an unaltered aggregate value for Income. However, the apportionments to the account categories differ.

8.3 Unnecessary use of Chart of Account Categories

On certain occasions, there may be instances where a chart of account categories that were previously utilized and are still alive is mistakenly employed. In order to mitigate this occurrence, it is possible to render them inactive.

In situations where there are two closely related categories, with one being mandatory, the Merge option can be employed. In the given illustration, two distinct kinds of chart of accounts are employed for Insurance Expense and Insurance Expense - General Liability.

Based on the given scenario, a consensus has been reached that solely the Insurance Expense is necessary. There is no need to make any modifications to the transactions as the utilization of the Merge function guarantees the consolidation of all transactions via both categories under a single heading.

The visibility of the Merge option is not apparent in any of the menus. The account in question will become accessible whenever the user decides to modify the account name, which is now not in use, in order to match the desired account name that they intend to retain.

In this context, the chart of account category pertaining to Insurance Expense - General Liability would be subject to modification, specifically involving the replacement of the existing designation "Name" with the more appropriate term "Insurance Expense." After the act of saving, users will be presented with the opportunity to merge their data.

The acceptance of the account merge would lead to a consistent monthly fee being applied to a singular category.

8.4 Accruals, Prepayments, and Deferred Income

Let us examine an illustrative case of a prominent advisory firm. The individuals are employed by a multinational corporation and are engaged in providing services to a client with a global presence. It has been recommended that they generate an invoice in anticipation of the upcoming quarter, amounting to £60,000.

Upon generating the invoice, the Profit and Loss report should promptly reflect an income of £60,000 for one month.

While the invoice was generated and settled in August, it would be inaccurate to record the entire income within a single month when preparing monthly reports. In the event that the organization did not have a substantial workload, it may potentially assert that August exhibited favorable performance, while September and October demonstrated comparatively lackluster results.

This scenario does not align with the typical business practice, as the business is receiving payment in advance for services that have not yet been rendered. Consequently, a portion of this revenue will require to be recognized at a later date to adhere to the principle of deferral. Implementing this measure will enhance the overall consistency in our accounting practices and ensure alignment with costs, particularly payroll expenses that are incurred in subsequent months.

In order to achieve the deferral of revenue, it is necessary to establish a suitable balance sheet account designated as Deferred revenue. Please proceed with creating one.

In order to maintain a monthly income of £20,000, it will be imperative to postpone a sum of £40,000 by the conclusion of August. It is necessary to generate a journal entry.

This entry will result in a decrease of £40,000 in the income figure as shown on our Profit and Loss statement. Once the Journal item has been saved and remains shown on the screen, users will have the opportunity to access the Reverse function located at the bottom of your screen. By choosing this alternative, a new journal will be generated with a date corresponding to the initial day of the subsequent month, wherein the credits and debits will be reversed.

The full sum can be reversed; however, in order to accommodate a two-month adjustment period, the values may be modified subsequent to selecting the Reverse option.

By accessing the inverted journal and navigating to the journal screen, users can save and display it. To produce a duplicate of the journal entry for October 1, 2021, users can pick the "More" option followed by "Copy" at the bottom of their journal screen.

The entries above depict the initial journal entry that was established with the purpose of eliminating the income figure from the Profit and Loss report. Subsequently, two additional journal entries were made to release the money.

If expenses are prepaid, it is necessary to apply the same rules. It is a prevalent practice for individuals to make payments for subscriptions and insurance coverage in advance for 12 months. Let us briefly examine some of the necessary preparations.

Adjusting prepayments

Occasionally, suppliers may issue invoices for products or services prior to the corresponding period. An illustration can be shown wherein an organization is presented with an invoice for a two-year subscription to a professional membership.

Upon inputting this individual invoice into the QuickBooks accounting software, a corresponding expense will be generated and promptly reflected within a one-month timeframe. The allocation of this expense should be done in a manner that ensures an equitable distribution of the charge across all pertinent months.

Assuming an initial charge of £2,400, the cumulative expenditure would be allocated to the subscriptions within one month. In order to achieve a consistent monthly cost of £100, adjustments would be necessary.

Prior to making adjustments for prepayments, sometimes referred to as prepaid expenses, it is imperative to ensure the appropriate chart of account category is established.

In the event of incurring an insurance expense amounting to £1,200 for 12 months, the initial course of action would involve the establishment of a journal entry to prepay either the entirety or 11 months' worth of the overall annual expenditure. In the event that the cost was accrued throughout a partial month, it may be advisable to allocate the expense based on a predetermined number of days. To ensure ease of transaction, we will make the payment for the complete year in advance. To complete this transaction, it is necessary to record a journal entry that debits the Prepayments account and credits the Insurance account for the full amount.

To facilitate the execution of a prepayment spanning 12 months, it would be advantageous to establish a recurring transaction. To initiate the process of generating a recurring transaction, please navigate to the gear icon and proceed to select the option labeled "Recurring transactions" from the LISTS menu.

To access the Recurring transactions section, users should navigate to the upper right corner of the screen and pick the New option. In this particular instance, it is imperative to choose a Journal Entry.

Within the upper section of a recurring template page, users can input a designated name for the template, choose its specific kind, and select from a range of interval possibilities.

Within the lower section of a recurrent entry screen, users have the option to select the method by which the entry will be generated on a monthly basis. In this given illustration, the recommended accounting entry would involve debiting the Insurance account and crediting the Prepayments account for an amount of £100 on each respective line.

While it is possible to generate recurring entries from the Recurring transactions list section, the Make recurring option is typically located at the bottom of manual data entry screens.

An initial journal entry of £1,200 is recorded, with a debit to the Prepayments account and a credit to the Insurance account. It is then followed by 12 further journal entries, each with a credit to the Prepayments account and a debit to the Insurance account, each amounting to £100. The Balance Sheet will be aligned, and a regular monthly insurance fee will be reflected on the Profit and Loss report.

The subsequent table presents a selection of balance sheet categories that can be established to modify revenue and expenditure, so enhancing coherence in our profit and loss reporting.

Account Name	Type	Detailed Type	Notes
Accrued income	Current assets	Other current assets	The initial journal will debit this account and credit income.
Prepayments	Current assets	Other current assets	The initial journal will debit this account and credit expenses.
Accrued expenses	Current liabilities	Current liabilities	The initial journal will credit this account and debit expenses.
Deferred income	Current liabilities	Current liabilities	The initial journal will credit this account and debit income.

How to record a payment?

In the context of financial management, the act of documenting a customer's payment is performed within the QuickBooks Online (QBO) platform. The Receive Payment window can be shown by various methods, which include:

Step 1: To initiate the process of receiving payment, users can navigate to the Create menu and subsequently choose the option labeled "Receive Payment."

Step 2: To initiate a new transaction, users may navigate to the Sales Transactions page and locate the New Transaction button. Upon clicking this button, users will be presented with a menu of options, one of which is the Payment selection.

Step 3: Under the Sales Transactions list, one can locate the specific invoice for which a payment is to be recorded and proceed to select the option "Receive Payment" found under the Action column.

If either of the initial two methods is utilized, QuickBooks Online (QBO) will present a Receive Payment window that does not contain any information. Next, a customer is chosen, and QuickBooks Online (QBO) proceeds to present a comprehensive overview of the customer's outstanding invoices under the Outstanding Transactions section, which is located at the lowermost part of the interface.

To initiate the payment process, navigate to the upper section of the screen and proceed to choose a Payment Method. Subsequently, opt for the specific account inside QBO where you wish to allocate the payment received from the customer. In the area labeled "Outstanding Transactions," it is advised to mark a check symbol next to each invoice that the payment made by the client is settling.

To record more client payments, navigate to the bottom of the Receive Payment window and select the "Save and New" option. Alternatively, you can click the arrow adjacent to "Save and New" and choose the "Save and Close" option.

What are the differences in outcomes when employing the third technique, which involves locating the invoice on the Sales Transaction list and selecting on Receive Payment button in the Action column? When utilizing the list, QBO will autonomously populate the customer's name, exhibit and choose the invoice selected from the Sales Transaction list inside the Outstanding Transactions area, and propose a payment amount.

Chapter 9: Real-Life Solutions and Visual Support

While utilizing QuickBooks Online, users may come across typical challenges that, although somewhat irritating, may be effectively addressed using real-life solutions and visual support.

9.1 Addressing User Frustrations and Concerns

Let us delve into a few of these problems and engage in a discourse on strategies for efficiently navigating them.

A prevalent concern is to **difficulties encountered with login credentials**. The inability to access one's QuickBooks Online account can elicit feelings of frustration. In the event that one encounters a lapse in memory regarding their password, it is reassuring to know that a viable solution exists. Specifically, a "Forgot your password?" hyperlink can be found on the login page, serving as a means to address this predicament. By selecting the designated option, QuickBooks Online will provide step-by-step instructions to facilitate the process of resetting your password. In the event that you continue to encounter difficulties, there exists an alternative to seek guidance by reaching out to QuickBooks Support.

Another potential problem that could arise is the **occurrence of transaction duplication**. This occurrence arises when an individual inadvertently inputs the same transaction repeatedly. In order to address this issue, it is recommended to navigate to your transaction history, discern the instances of duplication, and, after that, eliminate the surplus entries. QuickBooks Online provides users with a range of tools and filters that facilitate the identification and isolation of duplicate entries.

Issues related to banking and connectivity is frequently encountered. Occasionally, instances may arise where transactions fail to synchronize accurately with one's bank or when connectivity problems occur. In instances of this nature, one may attempt to disengage and subsequently reestablish the connection with their bank account. It is imperative to verify the proper operation of your bank's website and meticulously review your account credentials.

Data import challenges may occur during the transition from a distinct accounting system into QuickBooks Online. Ensuring accurate data formatting and adherence to QuickBooks Online's data import rules is crucial. It may be necessary to accurately align fields during the import procedure in order to correspond with the data structure of your prior system.

Among the most **commonly encountered difficulties pertains to the process of reconciling one's finances**. Discrepancies in reconciliation may arise as a result of transactions that have been either omitted or inaccurately recorded. In order to address this matter, it is advisable to conduct a thorough examination of both credit and bank card statements, ensuring that all transactions align with the corresponding records in QuickBooks Online. In the event that inconsistencies are identified, it is advisable to make appropriate modifications to the transactions in order to achieve a precise reconciliation of your accounts.

The task of monitoring expenditures and accurately classifying transactions can provide challenges at times. One may meet challenges when attempting to ascertain the suitable spending categories or when aligning transactions with the proper accounts. In order to address this issue, it is advisable to allocate sufficient time while inputting transactions and utilize the integrated tools provided by QuickBooks Online to effectively categorize and reconcile expenses with precision.

Another prevalent concern pertains to **difficulties encountered in the process of invoicing**. One may encounter difficulties throughout the process of creating invoices, including but not limited to inaccuracies in the omissions of essential information, invoice amounts, or complications arising from email transmission. In order to tackle this issue, it is advisable to verify the accuracy of invoice details, ensure the correctness of client email addresses, and utilize the preview functionality to thoroughly examine invoices prior to dispatching them to consumers.

Sales tax-related concerns may arise, particularly when a business operates in various tax jurisdictions. Accurate establishment and configuration of sales tax settings in QuickBooks Online are of utmost importance. It is advisable to periodically review one's tax settings in order to ensure adherence to evolving tax legislation.

Moreover, the management of inventory has the potential to elicit feelings of frustration. To address any inconsistencies in inventory levels, it is advisable to conduct periodic inventory audits in order to reconcile the tangible stock with the corresponding records in QuickBooks Online. This practice aids in the preservation of inventory precision.

Payroll issues can provide significant difficulties, as they encompass the remuneration and tax deduction aspects pertaining to your workforce.

It is imperative to verify the accuracy of your payroll settings and consistently examine payroll data in order to identify any inconsistencies or mistakes.

Occasionally, users may encounter **performance-related challenges** while utilizing QuickBooks Online, including instances of prolonged loading durations or system malfunctions. In order to resolve this issue, it is recommended to clear the cache and cookies of your web browser, utilize a browser that is compatible with the system requirements, and verify the stability of your internet connection. In the event that the issue persists, it is advisable to contact QuickBooks Support in order to obtain assistance.

In addition, it is imperative to **ensure the maintenance of accurate and current membership and payment details** for QuickBooks Online. Payment issues might disrupt access to the platform. Therefore, it is important to verify the validity of your payment method and ensure that the subscription is up to date.

Additionally, there may be **worries regarding data backup and security**. Regularly backing up the QuickBooks Online data is a prudent practice to mitigate the risk of data loss. QuickBooks Online offers a range of functionalities that facilitate the exportation and backup of data. In addition, it is advisable to employ robust passwords and contemplate the activation of multi-factor authentication as a means to augment the security measures implemented for your account.

Finally, **potential challenges may arise in relation to the integration and utilization of third-party applications**, particularly in cases where compatibility concerns or synchronization difficulties are encountered. It is vital to verify that the applications being utilized are compatible with one another and that they have been updated to the latest versions. If assistance is required, it is recommended to refer to the application's support documentation or reach out to their support team.

During the process of familiarizing oneself with QuickBooks Online, encountering these frequently encountered challenges is an inherent aspect of the learning process. It is important to keep in mind that individuals should not perceive themselves as isolated since there exists a multitude of resources that can be used to effectively address and overcome these difficulties. There are various avenues available for individuals to access knowledge and help related to QuickBooks, including contacting QuickBooks help, referring to user guides, or engaging with the QuickBooks community.

View these hurdles as valuable chances to improve your proficiency with QuickBooks Online. By successfully addressing prevalent challenges, individuals can enhance their proficiency as users, thereby enabling them to effectively utilize the extensive capabilities of this adaptable accounting platform to advance their corporate objectives. In order to maintain a positive outlook, exercise patience, and proceed with assurance, it is advised to persevere in one's pursuit of knowledge and experience in QuickBooks Online.

9.2 A Practical and Engaging Approach to Learning

QuickBooks has established itself as the predominant accounting software for businesses, catering to a wide range of entities, including self-employed individuals, small enterprises, and huge organizations. The straightforward and user-friendly design of the software facilitates efficient bookkeeping, tax management, and maintenance of accurate and current financial records for enterprises.

Although QuickBooks Online was specifically developed to have a user-friendly and straightforward interface, it is important to note that, like any software, there exists a certain level of complexity that users must navigate in order to effectively utilize the platform. It is noteworthy that individuals of all backgrounds possess the potential to attain proficiency in this application through the completion of a QuickBooks Online training course.

Advantages of participating in QuickBooks training

- **Alleviates feelings of being overwhelmed and effectively manages time:** Upon initial use of QuickBooks Online, it is important to undertake the appropriate procedures for establishing accounts and familiarizing oneself with the functionality inherent to the program. The process of acquiring knowledge may be both daunting and time-intensive. The provision of QuickBooks training significantly reduces the duration required for individuals to acquire proficiency in several features, including but not limited to invoicing and payment acceptance, report generation, expenditure tracking, and other related tasks. For individuals who are occupied with managing their own business or working as self-employed professionals, the time saved by QuickBooks training holds significant value.

- **Reduced mistakes, precise numerical data, and enhanced workflow efficiency:** A single error inside the bookkeeping system has the potential to disrupt the accuracy of numerical data and consequently generate reports that are not reliable. Certain issues might occur due to inadequate setup of the Chart of Accounts, incorrect association of items with accounts, duplication of transactions, and various other frequently seen faults in QuickBooks. The acquisition of QuickBooks training facilitates the acquisition of proficiency in utilizing the software in a precise manner, resulting in a reduction in errors and the generation of more precise numerical data. It, in turn, can significantly influence the process of generating informed financial judgments.

- **Maximize the utilization of the features and capabilities it offers:** QuickBooks offers a wide range of features and functionalities, including the integration of third-party applications and automated processes, which effectively streamline operations, enhance efficiency, and yield time-saving benefits while ensuring the precision and reliability of financial data. Numerous users may lack awareness regarding these valuable aspects; nonetheless, by undergoing QuickBooks training, one can effectively harness the software's complete range of capabilities and functionalities. The outcome is a heightened level of efficiency in the bookkeeping system.

Analytical index

Conclusion

QuickBooks is well recognized as a prominent and highly versatile accounting software solution specifically designed to cater to the needs of small businesses. The software offers a diverse range of product versions and lines that enable users to effectively monitor their income and expenses, as well as meet their tax requirements with ease.

QuickBooks Online, a small business accounting tool and app, enables users to effectively manage their business operations remotely and at any given moment. QuickBooks, a software platform utilized by a substantial client base of over 4.5 million users, provides a range of user-friendly solutions designed to facilitate efficient management of business operations. Users can effectively oversee their financial resources, generate and distribute invoices, monitor inventory levels, organize financial records, and facilitate payroll operations. QuickBooks Online offers enhanced organizational capabilities, time-saving features, and expedited payment processing through the integration of payment services. One notable advantage is the opportunity to evaluate the product without incurring any potential risks for 30 days.

QuickBooks is a software application that exhibits a high degree of user-friendliness, facilitating ease of use and comprehension for routine operational activities. The platform offers many projects that facilitate the management of contracts and projects while also enabling the computation of profits and earnings. Additionally, this feature enables users to compute the financial losses incurred from specific projects, thereby facilitating a comprehensive analysis of the factors contributing to the monetary deficit. The utilization of QB facilitates the organization and arrangement of various business instruments, such as purchase orders and delivery notes. In addition, it is possible to generate sales orders and acknowledge newly received orders from consumers.

Given its nature as accounting software, this particular software application offers comprehensive assistance in effectively managing various aspects of record-keeping for major corporations. Its functionalities encompass the creation of a chart of accounts, the establishment of product entries for pricing purposes, the organization of product inventory, and the meticulous recording of both the cost of purchase and the cost of sales. This tool will aid in the computation of the labor cost per hour for individual employees who are responsible for completing their assigned tasks inside designated contracts or projects that necessitate timely project completion for contractual services.

It is strongly recommended that individuals who have not yet registered for this exceptional software take the necessary steps to do so promptly.

Frame the qrcode and

download your BONUS here

Made in the USA
Coppell, TX
03 September 2024

36740435R00063